GHOST SIGN

Recent Titles by the Authors of *Ghost Sign*

AL ORTOLANI
Paper Birds Don't Fly
(New York Quarterly Books, 2016)

MELISSA FITE JOHNSON
While the Kettle's On
(Little Balkans Press, 2014)

ADAM JAMESON
#9 to Sallisaw
(Little Balkans Press, 2013)

J.T. KNOLL
Where the Pavement Ends
(2009)

GHOST SIGN

POEMS FROM WHITE BUFFALO

AL ORTOLANI
MELISSA FITE JOHNSON
ADAM JAMESON
J.T. KNOLL

Kansas City Missouri
Spartan Press

39 WEST PRESS

39 WEST PRESS
Kansas City, MO
www.39WestPress.com

SPARTAN PRESS
Kansas City, MO
www.SpartanPressKC.com

39 WEST
PRESS

Spartan Press

Copyright © 2016 by Al Ortolani, Melissa Fite Johnson, Adam Jameson, J.T. Knoll

All rights reserved. No part of this book may be reproduced, scanned, or distributed in any printed or electronic form, including information storage and retrieval systems, without permission. Please do not participate in or encourage piracy of copyrighted materials in violation of the author's rights. Please purchase only authorized editions.

First Edition: October 2016

ISBN: 978-0-9908649-6-7

Library of Congress Control Number: 2016953066

This book is a work of fiction. Names, characters, places, dates, and incidents are products of the authors' imaginations, or are used fictitiously, satirically, or as parody. Any resemblance to actual persons, living or dead, business establishments, events, or locales is entirely coincidental.

10 9 8 7 6 5 4 3 2

Design & Layout: Jason Ryberg, Will Leathem, j.d.tulloch
Edits: Jason Ryberg, Melissa Fite Johnson, Thomas Fox Averill, j.d.tulloch

39WP-13

CONTENTS

Introduction by Jo McDougall   1

Vienna Sausage by Al Ortolani

Summer Storm among the Strip Pits	5
Vienna Sausage	6
Midnight on the Camp 50 Water Tower	7
The Last Hippie of Camp 50	8
Hunting Toads	9
Nighthawks	10
Boxed In	11
The Junkyard Mechanic Finds His Voice	12
We Find Ourselves with Frogs	13
Bonnie the Clover Lady	14
Noodler's Advice to the Boys	15
Losing Our Paychecks at Bocci Ball on V-E Day	17
Coyotes	18
Hunting the Oldest Grave in the Town Cemetery	19
Shooting the Snapper	20
Some Moments Are Frozen	21
Muskrat Dump	22
Puttering	23
The Night of Bacon and Baseball	24
Another Tornado Warning	25
The Velvet Revolution Reaches Kansas	26
The Pre-Teen	27
Winter Solstice	28
Subsistence Farming	29
Tacitus Silent at Last	30
Thomas Paints a Fence	31
The Hermit of Euclid Street	32
Discovering Rose	33
Auction of Small Ghosts	34
Digging up the Septic Tank	35
Applause for Widow Audubon	36
English Class Angler	37

Second Rain	38
A History of Leaves	39
Hawk on the Practice Field	40
City Council Hires a Cannon	41
Sunday Ducks	42
Steam Engine 1023	43
Cemetery as Dog Park	44
Sullivan Shovels Snow at His Mother's Empty House	45
The Handyman Drinks	46
Mulligan	47
Polio Turtle	48
Viewing the Ballgame from the Hill	49
At the State 5A Football Playoff	50
Following Junkyard	51
Tony Paces the Sidelines	53
Mickey Mantle as a Longshot	54
Michael Hogard's Wake	55
A Strip Mine Resurgence	56

Backyard Universe by Melissa Fite Johnson

Summer Wedding	61
Ode to a Mason Jar	62
1931	64
Snapshot	65
A Postcard to My Husband in Kansas	66
Window Seat Haiku	67
Song for Kansas	68
After the Beep	69
High School Pep Band	70
Olive Street House Concerts, Pittsburg, Kansas	71
For the Girl at Kauffman Stadium	73
For the Woman at The Mall Deli	74
Walking Alone on North Broadway	75
Poetry Group	76
Watching My Husband Cook	77
Ode to Washing Dishes	78
Good Housekeeping	79
No One Could Agree Where to Bury Dad	80

Elegy for Three Local Businessmen	81
Linger	82
Lazy Sonnet	83
Sonnet for Rain	84
For Our Backyard Tree	85
Fire Pit	86
Pecan Picking	87
Resurrecting the Garden	88
My Grandparents at the Piano	89
At My Grandmother's Funeral	90
At My Student's Visitation	91
Teachers' Spring Break	92
Apologia for Not Wanting Children	93
Broody	94
Visiting the Dead	96

Small Town by **Adam Jameson**

Wild Red Berry Field	101
Splitting Wood on Robert Bly's Birthday	102
Watering the Oaks	103
Southpaw Catcher	104
Friday Night Lights	105
Saturday	107
Summer	108
Beaver Lake	109
Night before the Series	110
Lincoln Park	112
Fall Day	114
Frank Ferraro	116
Wind Storm	117
bottle rockets	118
Baseball Below the Light	120
Routine	122
I Always Take the Call	123
Twilight	125
Wading the River	126
Snow Geese	128
Lonestar Supper	129

Others Like Us by J.T. Knoll

Grandma's Smile	135
Quilting	136
Death Of A Railroad Man	137
Uncle Bill's Place	138
Lightning	139
Ballad Of Matt Knoll	140
Digging	142
Coal Miner Man	143
Edge Of The Pond	144
Driving	146
Letter To My Brothers	147
Driving In Winter	148
Sacred Heart	150
We Will Swim Naked Again	151
Listening	152
Others Like Us	153
two women in rosemary	154
The Riddle Of Fishes	155
awe	156
Duet	157
True Story	159
The Mall	160
Well, Some People Called It Psychedelic …	162
At the convenience store	165
it's funny	166
It Helps To Get It Out	167
Graveyard Shift At Ace's Truck Stop	168
Bicentennial Laundromat	169
Lazarus	170
Centering Prayer	172
Raiding The Kitchen At Assumption Abbey	173
You Gotta Call Me	174
december kansas twilight	176
Martyr To Whiskey	177
A son phones his father to say	178
For Fowler	179
News From The Front December 22, 2015	180
fatherhood	181

tai chi training continues	182
For Him	183
From Then On	184
Greeting The Fish	185
hitchhiking	186
Stairway To Brute	187
i'm not miro, nor chagall	188
i saw stevie pallucca	189
Borderline Song	190
Haircut	191
Running Away Down A Dead End Street	192

INTRODUCTION

I was an avowed Southerner when I came to Pittsburg, Kansas in the 1980s, to teach poetry and English at Pittsburg State University. A native Arkansan, I came to southeast Kansas from Monroe, Louisiana, where I had been teaching at what was then called Northeast Louisiana University. The two cultures could not have been more different.

I thought I'd never get accustomed to the relentless Kansas wind, the lack of lush foliage, and the absence of Southern fried catfish. But this unique region, occupying a lively corner of Kansas, soon won me over with its diverse and friendly populace, its democratic overtones, and its quirky mix of stoic, practical, and yet rebellious, don't-fence-me-in attitudes. (I also discovered its tasty fried chicken: the primary offering of two highly competitive and popular restaurants.) Despite learning, well into my occupancy, that a house I'd rented was atop an abandoned mining shaft and subject to collapse, the eleven years I spent in Pittsburg were among the happiest and most productive I've known.

Pittsburg had been a major coal-mining town in the 1920s and 1930s, attracting large and various ethnic groups from southeast Europe, many from the turbulent Balkans area, although there were a great many Italians who flocked to Pittsburg. The often belligerent, divisive spirit of the miners and the unpredictable politics of southeast Kansas earned the region the nickname *The Little Balkans.*

The four poets represented in this collection carry forward that same proud, independent spirit. They call themselves

White Buffalo, after a now-defunct café and coffee bar by that name in downtown Pittsburg. The bar had folded by the time I came to town, but its legend prevailed and remains to this day.

By all accounts, the White Buffalo was a popular and beloved place on Pittsburg's main street, Broadway. Offering both home and platform for writers, poets, artists, musicians, and friends, I'm told it fostered a spirit of challenge and diversity while offering warmth, inclusion, and community ... and quite possibly the best coffee in Pittsburg.

In that spirit of challenge and community, Al Ortolani, Melissa Fite Johnson, Adam Jameson, and J.T. Knoll give their poetry to us in *Ghost Sign* — a tribute to their native region, to both its ghosts and its very real characters and their stories.

This is honest work, lyrical and painful, joyous and sad. It is rooted in folk and mystery and place, informed by powerful imagery. Sunlight on the crater of a strip pit The shadow of an owl at Camp 50. Junkyard mechanics, railroad men, housewives. Ace's Truckstop. Coyotes, trains. A grandfather at a piano, plunking out Methodist hymns. Darkness gliding. Stories, all: misted, or sharp as winter rain.

I predict that readers of *Ghost Sign* will find in it their own ghosts, those indomitable, lost places and folk, brought back by the craft and passion of four poets who know how to remember.

— Jo McDougall

VIENNA SAUSAGE

AL ORTOLANI

*This book is dedicated to
Eugene DeGruson and Marjory Pease Sharp.
Thanks for your splendid guidance.*

Summer Storm among the Strip Pits

I have parked on a dump that overlooks
the water. Kingfishers slap surface,
dip and cut wide figure eights, lifting

like flapping hands into the sky.
Rain comes, peppering the surface
like thousands of winged insects, tapping

light fingers against the roof of my van.
Curtains blow. From the tops of poplars
I hear the wind moan, turning the alkali

over upon itself, the clay mixing
with gray shale, trickling
down from the tailings. The small soil

that runs between roots of a willow
clouds the vacant water
and spreads like the spawn of fish.

Vienna Sausage

Crows ride on wind. A deep strip trench cuts easterly into the earth, surrounded by shale, dumped tires, scrub sumac, scar tissue. Strip pits erupt and fold like proud flesh above a wound. Sitting with pen and notebook, I turn my body, readjust my ass against the cool gray slag. Ground water seeps through my denim. Families on the way between Mindenmines and Crowburg peer at me like some carnival barker, the one who leads them into the tent with the two-headed deer and the child with the white eyes. Tomorrow, someone will push a battered car into a green pool of alkali. A plaid couch will be dumped beside the railroad tracks and burned. Teenagers will dance around it, spilling Natural Light and passing reefer. They will drink, cuss, and toast brotherhood in the rising sparks, the glowing coals. Coyote tracks edge the slag pile, circling the mud, spotting the day like smudge marks, connecting the periphery where man and nightfall link arms. At midnight they are heard among the sycamores, yelping, peeling their enthusiasm for the trash lot, nosing cans of pork and beans and half-eaten Vienna Sausage in wine sauce. Voices are on the wind, somewhere with the crows. Four walnut horses with red jacketed riders appear, picking their way across the section. They weave amid the dumps and then out into the reclaimed grassland. The horses toss, pull against the reins like storms.

Midnight on the Camp 50 Water Tower

An owl drops out of the dark struts
of the water tower, and swoops
down across the tops of the trees.
He circles the water tower, scattered
stars at his wing. Mercury-vapor farm lights
wheel below him. They are like small stars,
clustered around the old deep shafts, constellations
with names like Crowburg, Frogtown,
Breezy Hill, and Ringo; they are as
quiet as the night
below the shadow of the owl.

The Last Hippie of Camp 50

The mulberry set right plunk
Above your clothesline is no problem.
Someday you'll crank the yellow McCullouch
And drop back the limbs
One by one until the sun falls through

Flat and warm as a flannel cake.
A late freeze hints in the sunset,
Your wife works late to cover the tomatoes
With plastic jugs from Oldham's Dairy,
You consider painting a sign that reads

Spare Volkswagen Parts, but smoke
White Owl Miniatures instead,
Watching the last sun capture another jug
And stroking your untrimmed beard
Into the shape of an arrowhead.

Hunting Toads

When you are lonely for something
you can't quite put your finger on,
wake the children at midnight,
take them outdoors before the front porch,
push aside the lantana and hollyhock,
and there, like dark globs of mud,
you'll find toads. Startled,
they'll pop against the clapboards
of your home like air-gun corks.

Your children will fight moths
for safe space
inside the flashlight's beam,
but you'll keep pushing them out into the darkness.

Go, you tell them, *look into the shadows.*
Separate the geraniums.

Hunt toads.

The children squeal,
stomping their feet into the hoe-broken earth,
air guns popping into the vanilla moonlight.

Nighthawks

Inside your body is a wish
when on hot summer nights
you pull a mattress
through the window and lie
like a smoldering cigarette
on the rubberized roof.
Something inside
wants to reverse gravity,
to unpin, and spin away
weightless from the city.

Inside your body is a wish
that joins with nighthawks
beyond the coaxial cables,
stainless flues and smudges of neon,
beyond the dizzying spires
of steeple and antenna
where street lights fog
and supper clubs
wisp away like smoke.

Inside your body
white-streaked wings beat
up from your chest,
your throat, your mouth,
and plunge through your teeth,
releasing from the dry crackle
of skin and bone,
your spark.

Boxed In

Inside the cardboard
beside the patio fence,
the small, wire-necked
turtle, rescued

from the passing lane
on US 69, scratches
and claws against
the fibers of the box.

I hear him clearly
above the hedge clippers
that whir among
the manicured shrubs.

After dark, I drive
the roadside down Drywood Creek.
Stopping among the cattails,
I lift him from his

beer-box, moonlit nails
clawing the night air,
straining for the freedom
of wild onion and sage.

For a moment,
after he has pushed
between the reeds and grasses,
I listen for some

tumbling of the stream,
the owl call, the deer
that jumps the fence
downstream.

The Junkyard Mechanic Finds His Voice

He tried to sing,
to release the music that welled up inside
like a clouding seltzer. But when his mouth opened,

scrap iron grated across pickup beds.
He grew still, confused by his awkwardness,
shied like a lizard

and fell back into the bottle, retreating
into the shadows of the yard lamp.
He drew an eye upon the others

who sang in the mercury vapor, slapping cheap guitars
and pitching songs into the night
like horseshoes. In his truck cab

he kept a cobalt revolver, wrapped in a red grease rag
and stuck below the driver's seat.
On the drive home, he would aim it

between passing headlights.
He'd sing into the soupy air,
his voice clear and familiar.

We Find Ourselves with Frogs

Consider frogs
as they swell with air, the injustice
they must suffer to find themselves

so suddenly large and out of text
with hunting, and all for the sake
of love song, some throaty bellow

into the midnight air. A frog's world
must be one of sudden change, expanding
the way they do to find lovers,

the quick tongue held by stones,
mouth and throat
swollen, lungs and belly a gasping

encumbrance.

Bonnie the Clover Lady

As children we'd watch her plop her laundry basket
below the pink mimosa
and walk through the yard, soft-eyed, head tilted

into invisible currents.
Knowing we watched,
she'd stoop to earth and brush her hand across the grass
as if it were a shock of hair. She might be skimming
scum from the surface of a pond,
so she could peer into the water clearly
as if it were a mirror.

Bonnie could find four leaf clovers clumped in any lawn.

They grew that way in bunches,
and where you found one, you could find two.

It was the first find that kept you hacking across the sandlot,
pressing your nose into failure.

The clover lady had the knack like few do
for seeing the ripple of four in an ocean of three.
As kids, we figured that it was a talent
coming with age, this gift
for side-stepping disappointments.

Noodler's Advice to the Boys

They's here, he says, biggest damn catfish
you ever laid eyes on,
can take a man's arm and peel it back to bone.

He stands, creaks upright out of the Neosho,
barrel-chested and raw from sun,
jabbing us with his grin.
Here, you try.

We ain't crazy. So everyone laughs,
backs off like shad.

He gurgles a Schlitz,
wallers down to water level,
river popping into his armpits,
feels for the catfish hole. Sinks
deep to the shoulder.

Nothing, he curses. Not a jesus h nibble.
Rises to his knees.

No luck today, boys.
His eyes wander upstream like homemade spinners.
They's deeper, I suppose.
Closer up to the dam,
but a man's crazy to noodle those cat holes.

His eyes widen.
Wrinkles erupt from his forehead like finger-thick worms,
cats as big as a man. Put your fist
down one of them throats, they clamp on tight
and you don't come up.

I know. I've seen 'em
stretched on the bottom as lazy as shadows.
Too damn big to swim.

He shakes the beer can like a coin bank,
tosses it to the rocks.

In this life, boys,
a man's got to know the difference between
fishin' and gettin' fished.

Losing Our Paychecks at Bocci Ball on V-E Day

The Italians from the mining camps
Lined the railroad ties in their baggy pants
And clean white undershirts, drinking *dago red*
From plastic cups. They hustled us with
A brash bocci ball and finessed our slender wallets
With coal-darkened wagers. We were kids from town
Where the machinery for the deep shafts was built,
Where widows and daughters bought steamship tickets
For home, where their fathers had trouped
On Saturdays to trade bathtub gin for trouble.
By late evening, when the music
Began to drift down from the band dome,
They leaned on the hoods of their Fords to eye
Our bare-legged girls, and grin their wide, toothy smiles.

Coyotes

I was out trying a Volkswagen
for my daughter, when I see these two
coyotes dipping through the fence row
and tailing like two bullets of wind
across a green pasture.

I bounce behind the wheel
of this yellow Bug, churning up the road's dust,
thinking thoughts of rust and end play
and new-bled brakes, and I know
they never lift an eye

from my noise. Well, I'd honk
and throw a hearty wave
but the horn's dead, and the road
jogs way right
so I plow ahead, hands at ten and two,

the sudden coyotes
two specks in a farmer's field
already disappearing.

Hunting the Oldest Grave in the Town Cemetery

was acclaimed as one among many
great history lessons,
completed by the third grade class
during the Kansas Centennial.
The class waded among headstones
drowned in fescue
and crawled below the junipers to etch
newsprint with charcoal.
Classmates visited the old fort,
and balanced on the ramparts,
catching the faraway cries of stragglers
from the skirmish on Cow Creek. Others
in tilling the garden
turned horseshoes between Tom's tomatoes,
unearthing a bit more
of the Iowa City blacksmith.
North at the natural ford,
some searched the unplowed pastures
for buffalo wallows and military trail wagon ruts.
The class dug a hole below the flagpole
and planted a time capsule
with their full names signed in pencil
on a scroll of Big Chief.
They would each be one hundred
and nine when they dug it up,
except for the new kid from Missouri
who'd been held back a grade.
He'd be one hundred and ten.

Shooting the Snapper

The first sun snags him
like a fishing line, netting his soup bowl
shell, his razor claws,
his slate eyes peering
with dim curiosity down
his queer, hooked snout.
He waits, a phalanx, beside the flood brush,
a guardian of prehistoric DNA.

When the Crawford boys stop their pickup
and pull a .22 from behind the seat,
he doesn't edge into the bean rows
but rises on powerful, bowed legs,
suddenly all piss and spit. The boys
circle to within a few steps, aiming deep
into his bone-encased brain.

His leathered neck strains
with the one plan decoded. Hissing
at the leveled blue barrel,
he snaps beautifully at
the exploding sun.

Some Moments Are Frozen

The sun's finally out, but between
the fallen crocus and the trash truck
are thousands of twinkling ice
crystals. I'm fixing the bird
feeder, restringing a nylon cord
to the sawed-off limb, letting the
weight of the seed pull it taut
to where it pendulums in the wind
of sparrows. Nothing in this moment
lends itself to words.
Even if I had waited a lifetime,
no one would speak.
The neighbor lady would pull
shut her curtains before noon
and the dog would sit sullenly
in the flower bed, her head
like a spade
raised over the dark soil.

Muskrat Dump

The afternoon sunlight
warms my back
while woodpeckers drum
hollow limbs in the tree-
tangled dumps. A few
remaining persimmons
darken. Wind rustles
the brown undergrowth;
leaves clatter and snag
on bunchberry vines.
I lie among them like
a branch, fallen
and comfortable with decay.

The pit's green water
crests a canoe, red keel
creasing the surface
like the snout of a muskrat
stretching for the coal slag
shoreline. Overhead
the blue sky is interrupted
only by thoughts
of sleep,
and amazingly, out
of the scrub oak
a December butterfly,
as fragile and temporary as daylight.

Puttering

    dissolves into the soil.
The hat on the fencepost
   slouches in
     the midnight rain
       like a dream
     collapsed
     and fallen in.
   The brim is
  permanently funneled,
a rain spout
above the herb garden.
The maze of bricks
  lifted from the patio,
    reset
     in the circular whirl
      of a wheel;
      cilantro, comfrey,
       chamomile,
         spin outwards
          away from the bird-
       bath hub.
      Even our footprints
       dissolve like the summer,
      the crows
       thieves in the corn.

The Night of Bacon and Baseball

When the wind blew the power lines
Into the shelter house, it showered the park
With pigeon feathers. Sparks popped
And snapped and the smell of cooked bird
Rose with the blue smoke into the light poles.
Of course, all was pitched
Into darkness, and the boys playing baseball
Began to slide into whatever base
Was closest. An old woman frying bacon
On Martin Street cursed her new electric stove
And wished her son had never insisted
On the change from gas. The bacon
Bubbled and sizzled down in the heated grease
Until it was somewhat cooked, but she
Tossed it angrily into the trash. Finally,
Lightning cracked and the boys on the ball diamond
Were hurried into the dugouts by the coaches
Where they sat with their gloves on their laps
Swinging their legs and watching the field
Disappear in a torrent of rain. Two teenagers
Who had escaped the bleachers and slipped
Into a Ford Taurus saw this as an opportunity
To unleash zippers and buttons. Fast Ernie,
The dog, stretched on his hind legs
To nose the bacon from the trash can,
The rain water streaming down his back
In freshets of grime and fleas.
The electric company
Had a truck on the way, two workers,
One of them smoking a cigar, the other tuning
The Royals game on the radio. Cats skulked
In the shrubs for the rain to let up.
They licked their lips and sharpened their claws.

Another Tornado Warning

Grandpa puts Grandma in the closet with a flashlight,
a bottle of water, and a video poker game.
By and by, he joins her
although he has to sit on a stepladder.
He closes his eyes and listens to Larry
the white cockapoo whimper
below Grandma's chair.
As the storm builds, Grandpa opens
the closet door. The television casts a pale blue
eye across the living room. Grandma sleeps
and Larry shivers with each roll of thunder.
The St. Louis Cardinals are up by two runs
and Albert Pujols is stepping to the plate.

The Velvet Revolution Reaches Kansas
for Henrik Christensen

Otto lived in a house boat on the Neosho River.
Some said he was a pot farmer in hiding. Mostly,
he drank cases of Pilsner and floated
the corked bottles on limb lines.
On cold nights a foggy light frosted his window;
blue smoke twisted free from stove chimney.
A gang plank extended to the shore,
and a beaten trail curved upwards to the county road.
But that was before something serious happened
and the trail was overrun with kudzu,
the plank sinking into the river. This occurred
right after the Berlin Wall collapsed. Neighbors renewed
their interest, and wagered his career failed
with the Cold War, a disconnect no doubt
from the CIA. He spoke Czech, you see,
received letters, addressed in a clear feminine hand
from Prague of all places. When the letters stopped,
KGB agents, identified by their nondescript Renaults,
crept slowly up the county road,
searching for the path overgrown with green.
The truth of the matter (from a Bohemian source)
claimed Otto had taken to writing
children's stories about talking cats.
They were being published in the Czech Republic
under the *nom de plume* of a beautiful
young blonde named Freda Horst.

The Pre-Teen

Home from the fifth grade's
annual bird walk to Lincoln Park,
my daughter flowers
with new-fired interest
in the order of things.
She mocks the quiver
of the meadowlark's *spring-of-
the-year*,
sketches the breast to breast
climb of wrens
throughout mid-air, imagines the bullsnake
as he smoothes and stretches
out of another skin.

From the porch steps
it is the voices of boys
who mill about our door,
green as cornsilk,
unpolished, immature.
While my daughter,
fresh and supple
as willow,
intoxicated easily with blossom,
still dreams of mockingbirds
white-winged
as she topples eleven.

Winter Solstice

The neighbor woman walks out in a red bathrobe,
stooped against the cold, arms folded protectively to her.
She opens the door of the shed and a dozen or more chickens
fly out like leaves blown by a power mower. They swirl

about her legs and then are quickly tossed out of sight
around the edge of the garage. The woman hurries inside
to the coffee she left on the windowsill.
Long bars of sun flex across the shadows. The chickens

mill about the lawn, pecking the sunlight from the roots
of the zoysia. Her coffee, fanning a halo of steam
above the sill, rises in the light of the sink;
a small metal chain connects to the bulb.

Subsistence Farming

The kitchen door
 swings wide
 and his wife appears,
  her arms folded against the chill.
  Snow makes the green
 so very green,
and she points to the squirrel-ear lettuce
cropping in bed rows.
He flails a hand as much to heaven
 as to snow, Cold
 will set us back.
 But the curve of her
   warmth comes to him
    and he returns to the house.
     Words fail him in love; they rust
      like garden tools
       and clank against his teeth.
        A well-oiled hoe. Soft
         soil for carrots. Red
          worms and mulch.
           She opens her arms to reply,
           Turnips and radishes,
            potatoes pulled
            from dirt.

Tacitus Silent at Last

The opossum digs through the trash
in the back of the house. The man
hears him tearing paper bags
and nosing cans of ravioli from the night's supper.
A bottle clunks against the concrete sidewalk
and he recalls the wine turned to vinegar,
poured down the sink last week.
Tacitus the terrier yelps, scratching at the kitchen door
and clicking his nails against the linoleum.

He rolls half a Xanax in cheese,
and drops it in the dog's bowl.
He slips open the study window and eases out
onto the porch roof, gingerly settling the Johnny Walker
against the familiar shingles. He has duct taped
his Eveready flashlight to the stock of his son's
BB gun. The opossum settles.
The man fears he has waddled off across the alley.
So he waits, staring at the remains of his marriage
strewn down the sidewalk. Now, with Tacitus silent,
maybe he can hear. Any of those paper bags
could hide the truth.

Thomas Paints a Fence

A praying mantis the size of Tom's fingernail
creeps an inch from the new paint. He takes
the tip of his putty knife and lifts it
free before it's engulfed in latex, imprisoned

like a mosquito in Baltic amber. Lightly,
he blows it into the blades of pampas grass.
When he spreads another brush load,
a second and a third mantis

ride up over the lip of the post.
He doesn't remember seeing a nest
so he begins to search the length of fence,
brush in bucket, hands on knees, head tilted,

eyeing every thorn of weathered wood.
When he shakes out his brush to begin again,
each stroke begins with a quiet breath,
a fingertip in a wound.

The Hermit of Euclid Street

In a three story hermitage
on Euclid Street, one light shines.
At dawn daylight hastens
about the doorstep; you,
quiet in the back
kitchen, brighten

junk mail
from the Rosicrucians, ordering

at last two books from their list
of an esoteric thousand.
You call to me
from your window: a problem

with the Upanishad,
a difficulty in untying one verse,
a snag in the long hair
of your Persian cat,
a window that allows too much
of your quiet light out

into an intersecting street.
I mention in all candor
a friend who knows something
about philosophy. He might add
to your concern. Even though
he lives but a few houses away,
you tell me to have him write, to
keep at length from your door, to
mail his ideas. You wave
as the curtain closes,
your neighbors drowning
in a flood of suggestions.

Discovering Rose

Not even the oldest neighbor (two
were interviewed)
recalled what this fringe of daffodils once outlined.
So for the sake of history, they invented
a plausible, potting shed
with stacks of dank, clay pots,
stacked one inside the other,
leaning (impossibly) into
a shadow of tomato stakes, some
tied with nylon stockings.

A pair of cotton gloves, pinked
with a faded, blossom print,
quietly feminine, caressed the lip
of a watering can.
Tools (industriously)
hung on pegboard:
the small spade and the weeding claw
and the iron crowbar for poking
holes for bulbs. All were connected
(poignantly) with cobwebs
in a galvanized bucket.

On the upper shelves, beyond
the curiosity of her cats, stood
brown bottles and dusty cardboard
labeled Poison. A sleepy
wasp flitted in the doorway breeze.
She kept a fence (defensively), probably
of painted wire.
Below the fly-specked window squatted
a bushel basket, half-filled
with the neighbor children's stained baseballs
and scuffed plastic Frisbees.

Auction of Small Ghosts

Colonel Banjo the auctioneer
sets up a table of glassware:
green depression, portrait bowls,
hand-painted chocolate pitchers,
a Limoges hair receiver;
and then along the hedgerow, he lines
end tables, a marble-topped dresser,
slag floor lamps, a mahogany hall tree.
Next to the basement steps squats
a bushel basket of deer antlers,
a stoneware crock of crocus bulbs,
a broken Nu Grape clock, hand tools, milk jugs,
the headlights of a Bel Air,

a cardboard box for the mortician
who collects windup toys,
one for Rose from the junk shop
who buys chipped McCoy,
another for the florist who sells buttons
and postcards on eBay. They bid
for connection to what has passed.
Mr. Garrison the biology teacher
sprays chigger repellent on his ankles
before walking the high grass
to the barn. He shoulders
a flat of faded photographs,
small ghosts smiling through sepia.
Draped over the stock fence,
Colonel Banjo displays
the toe-holed quilt the family
wrapped Terry the schnauzer in
the night he died of heart worm.

Digging up the Septic Tank

Repairing the septic tank
in summer heat
is serious work for an old man;
his neighbors shout
from air-conditioned Fords
that he's crazy to be out in this.
Waving his iced tea,
he takes a cut of bailing wire
and sinks it to find soft soil;
several times he clips the spool,
narrowing a circle until he strikes
the top of the tank.
He rings the perimeter
between virgin rock and turned soil
with wire spears; he squares
a folding chair
next to the garden. With a spade
and a sharp shooter,
kept oiled in the barn, he parcels
the repair down to concrete and tar.
His eyes rest on prize
tomatoes, rooted into the
lateral's current, untouched
by drought.

Applause for Widow Audubon

Mud-deep in her husband's boots,
she spills sunflower seeds
into the feeder. Starlings
dot the lawn, truculent and greedy.

She slaps the metal scoop
against the trash lid, shakes
a can of WD-40
and sprays the feeder pole
to slow the squirrels.
Tonight's applause
is late for Widow Audubon;
she works alone,
December shadows barring
the lawn like a cage.

Wheel of Fortune, her
favorite, spins through
the kitchen window, flickers
off a 50 gallon storage drum,
galvanized against rust, tightened
against mildew. Once
they had time, the two of them
for television, for sunflower seeds
protected, they thought,
forever in a metal can.

English Class Angler

...our sudden thought
of the water shining
under the morning fog

from a poem of Wendell Berry
checked out as a writing prompt
from the school library

by a boy who'd rather be casting
sleek monofilament from his johnboat
than reading.

He writes of strip pit water at dawn,
the wash of silver
that cascades from fish leaping

for mosquitoes
as the dark brightens.
Pole whipping thin light, he stirs

the classroom with quips, casts,
waits for poetry to strike,
to break surface like bass.

Second Rain

The 17 foot Grumman
rests on sawhorses
behind the garage at Golden Age.
Mrs. Vacca's mutt
anchors the frayed blue tarp
in rain storms. The water
that drips off the roof
splatters along the keel
and runs in small rivers
to the paws of the dog. He ignores
the mourning doves
bathing in puddles, tossing
the storm from their wings
in a thin spray. The canoe's
aluminum sidewalls
drum all morning in the new rain,
a hollow bass,
drenched with June.

A History of Leaves

The leaves are so wet, they
roll up in layers like scrolls
under the pitchfork.
Each veined with a thin,
cuneiform message from
the past season.
A woman calls her children
to brandish an army
of rakes and blue tarpaulins;
she cheers
as they load the sodden leaves
into the pickup bed.
Their demeanor is not that
of antiquarians or bibliophiles
hushed over books in a quiet hall.
They dance in the spotted sunlight
between the empty branches,
between the empty tines
that claw the air.
They sing new songs on the
road to the dump.

Hawk on the Practice Field

The edge of town is not squared,
its carpentry wearied, twisted
as milkweed in January, each season
tugged by gravity, dissolved by rain,
blown by wind. Change is built on conflict,
the smallest bulb, blackened by freeze,
buoys the tulip above death. It screws
through the packed dirt. The hawk
on the goal post leans
tentatively toward the field mouse
in the uncut grass; the dagger
of wing, the clench of talons.

City Council Hires a Cannon

Tonight, I went running, following
the sound of the starling cannon, fired
from below the trees at Lakeside Park.
Above Jefferson Street starlings
circled in growing flocks. They swept
the tops of the elms. The gun pounded,
growing louder, less familiar.
Starlings rose and fell with each report,
pushed to distant trees
by a force they could not fathom.
I ran through puddles from the evening's rain,
the reflection of the sky
splashing beneath my shoes.

Sunday Ducks

Three ducks walk the parking lot
at Braum's Ice Cream. They round
the corner of the exit drive, hugging
the curb to forage asphalt. The drake
scans traffic on Broadway, unconcerned
about his distance from Lakeside Park.
He is drawn by syrup, sugar cone,
vanilla wafer. He stops,
pulls his yellow feet below his wings
and sits in the traffic lane. The hens follow,
assured by confidence, webbed poise
amid blaring horns, waffle crumbs,
strawberry yogurt spreading like snowmelt.

Steam Engine 1023

Your daughters dig out the sled
and lean it inside the garage, readied
for the overpass at Schlanger Park.
Lamp lit windows hang against
the house like flat screen TVs.
By nightfall, goose feathers loosen
from the clouds and drift in the gray streets.
You step out to the porch and breathe
woodsmoke from a neighbor's chimney,
and in the taste of cold
you know today's disappearing, your memories
sculptured in snow. Tomorrow,
a girl with a red scarf flies down the overpass,
her steel runners singing, cutting
toward the chain link. For years
the old locomotive has waited
at the bottom of the hill
for the fastest sleds, daughters like yours
pumping their fists.

Cemetery as Dog Park

Sunday afternoon—a cold gray nips
the air—the same gray that drove us
as boys to the cemetery, where sheltered
in the evergreens, protected from the wind,
we planned our futures, one dog
or another panting at our feet. Fifty
years is a long time for boys, an impossibility
for dogs, a big nothing for the sun. Even
the cold, creeping slowly into our thighs,
is as temporary as juniper berries, bagworms,
sprawling limbs. Memory comes and goes
as we count the winters, the dogs that
licked their balls, chewed our shoes,
ran into traffic like happy fools.

Sullivan Shovels Snow at His Mother's Empty House

Tossed with salt, the pavement

blues up like a vein in the wrist.
The house wears a hairdresser's cut—
newspaper cancelled, mail rerouted, lights

timed to follow her make-believe journey—
kitchen to bedroom, bedroom to bath,
somnolent, blank as Ambien.
The furniture sits as was left, chairs pushed

to the Formica table, digital photos
flashing smiles below the clock, the television
clicking on at six, off at ten—

the philodendron watered.

The Handyman Drinks

in the shade of a sweet gum.
His saw is plugged into an orange
extension cord which is fed
through the storm window
and into the house. Hammer,
nails, tool belt are scattered
like leaves on the new porch.
Miller Lite bottles shine with
a dull amber around his feet. The beer
has gone down too easily, one
after the other. He loads
the scrap lumber into the
back of his truck and drives
home on dirt roads—
Kansas sun angled through
the trees, strip pits lush
and overgrown in
drunken green. He drives fast,
eating carry-out chicken,
tossing the bones out the window
like pleasant abstractions,
road dust a billowing curtain.
He stops at a jeep trail
slanted over a slag dump, eroded
and rutted from neglect.
He unloads tongue-and-groove
and ripped two-by-fours. He pitches
them with the beer bottles
into a tangle of briar. Cicadas
build in the deepening woods.

Mulligan

When I was a kid, my grandmother
used to take me on walks
along the railroad tracks near her house.
After summer storms, branches
littered the rail bed. I used them
as baseball bats. Sometimes
tramps emerged from the dumps,
scarecrows knocking backdoors
for handouts. Grandmother
said they were like deadwood,
pruned by wind. She kept

the door locked, even in the daytime.
They camped, trains in—trains out,
by the clay quarry. Some slept
in the stacks of drainage pipes, others
in brush lean-tos. She wouldn't
walk with me into the hobo jungle.
I had met one close-up before
on the sidewalk outside of the Pla-mor.
He was a bum, but he'd tapped
me on my ball cap with his knuckle,
said, "Hey pal," as he passed.

From the trestle, we watched them
knotted over their orange fire, sharing
mulligan from a coffee can.
Grandmother said, "Poor things,"
and then she hurried me home.

Polio Turtle

It took ten cents to ride the bus uptown
and then a penny to give the elevator boy
(although he was a man) to take us to the fourth
floor of the Professional Building. The doctor
charged $5 a visit, but he let Mom pay it out
over time. She said that with seven kids
the doctor's account was revolving. Afterwards,
we walked to Chubb's where she bought
me a six-cent Green River in a paper cone.
Not counting the doctor's bill, Mom and I could spend
the day for 17 cents each. Lunch at Woolworth's
was out of the question, so was the Five and Dime
unless I needed a shot or stitches. Then I could
choose from anything under 49 cents.
Polio closed the city pool that summer, and
the following fall all the school kids
were fed sugar cubes. I wondered
what an iron lung would earn me at Kress's.
When my best friend got sick,
Mom broke down and bought me a painted turtle.
He crawled on colored pebbles
below a plastic palm tree.

Viewing the Ballgame from the Hill

There is a haze above the park tonight.
The soprano cheers of young females
carry across Cow Creek, hailing
the ring of the aluminum bat.
It is a small town game, flat
with boots and miscues and failed
runs to the plate, but the midnight halo
of the diamond lights presses the black
pitch of the night up away from the crowd.
The dust that rises with each lead
wisps easily into the tobacco-stained dugouts.
A cloud-white batter steps into the box
and pumps enough practice swings
to lift the lights, momentarily free of moths.

At the State 5A Football Playoff

Is there any reason why on this evening,
which is more rain than mist,
a young man's exertion should pour upwards
like the smoke children imagine rising from dragons?
Between two rows of colored helmets, the knee bends
and mud-dripping face masks wait
to vanish as clouds
guffawed into the night.
They limp home, energies spent,
the thump and thud of the evening
swirling in the mud holes of their prints.

Following Junkyard

My father, as athletic trainer,
let me tag the sidelines
with a small plastic doctor's bag.

He loved the scrappers, tough guys
busting for a fight—my favorite
was Junkyard, Vietnam bound,

half-concussed, fingers taped
in make-shift splints. As free safety,
Junkyard was the forlorn hope.

Small, but wiry, he launched
his body like a bola, like a sling,
like a helicopter prop.

I followed Junkyard all season

with rolls of tape, nylon-wrapped
smelling salts, and a strange
plastic corkscrew which

when wedged between teeth
could pry open a locked jaw.
Junkyard wasn't far from

joining the punch drunk and
selling popcorn in the stands.
He should have taken up badminton,

miniature golf, or watercolor.
Quit, Dad said, before you feel
as bad as you look. I dropped salt pills

into Junkyard's paw. He winked at me
behind his facemask and grinned
with his toothless, baby-pink gums.

Tony Paces the Sidelines

The word on the street was that Tony
had been a genius, a lawyer maybe,

but scarlet fever had cooked his brain; synapses
had melted into gruel. What was left

kept him shackled, tongue on a spoon
slurping syllables, eyes watery,

rheumatic on game days. He chewed
Union plug, spit on the grass, hands

pocketed with notepads and pencils.
The administration complained about Tony,

a village idiot on the sidelines, ragtag,
unseemly for a conference powerhouse.

He displayed his field pass on a lariat
looping his neck. Each year the same:

coaches planned, posed scenarios,
consulted cigars. Tony paced

the twenty-yard line, his flap of brain,
inflamed with offense, moving the chains.

Mickey Mantle as a Longshot
for Doc Grimaldi

One night Mike and I blew our allowances
on packs of baseball cards. It paid off. I found
a Mickey Mantle wedged behind the gum. Mike
unwrapped a Roger Maris. We danced in the shade

of the elm behind the concessions. Grimaldi
and Ferns were coming up to bat. We ran
behind the left field fence with about 20 other
Pony Leaguers and waited for the long ball.

A homer, returned to the scorekeeper, earned
a snow cone or two more packs of cards, maybe
a Whitey Ford or a Yogi Berra, maybe a chance
to keep collecting behind the backstop.

With each pitch the crescendo of cicadas rose.
If the ball dropped over the fence, we knew
we were in for a fight. We teased the hitters
with chatter. We chomped our now tasteless gum.

Time hung in the lights like a slow curve.

Michael Hogard's Wake

The happy hour from Chubb's Bar
kneels shoulder to shoulder: dominoes

with bare fists, stiff shoes, and spiked
pocket hankies. Rosary beads

rattle against the pew like knuckles.
The prayers, memorized at St. Mary's,

have grown unfamiliar. They recite them
as slurs of inarticulate vowels,

growled *RRRs*, and sputtered *Ts*. Sister Anna
still watches, frowning as their

butts rest on the pew like a barstool,
a first sign of the devil's sloth, and then

the second back at Chubb's, when Tom Burns
twirls his finger for another round.

A Strip Mine Resurgence

In her charcoal a catfish
wallows in the shallows,
curved like a gurkha
and knifed between arrowhead plant
and water lilies.
The afternoon sunlight flattens
a warm plastic sky
stippled with dragonflies.
The artist sits on a shoal of slag,
Tevas splattered with grainy muck,
notebook on her knees.
Each sketch is young with contradiction,
heron wings and beer cans,
glittering glass, a fishing line,
kingfishers darting against the pit water.

A wand of cane, a cattail
caught by a blackbird, the chocolate
shine of the water turtle's shell
shimmers like a window of wavy glass,
and she is pulled by the heat
into a languor, her charcoal
fading along the edges of the paper
into a sort of haze, the heat
smoothing sharp lines and softening
the morning's muscle. Suddenly,
she is lifting her Peruvian skirt
and wading into the reflection of cottonwoods
cool against her thighs.

AL ORTOLANI

Al Ortolani's poetry and reviews have appeared in journals such as *Rattle, Prairie Schooner, New Letters, The Writer's Almanac,* and the *New York Quarterly,* and his poems have been nominated for the Pushcart Prize and Best of the Net. He has published several collections of poetry, including *His Waving Mustard in Surrender* (NYQ Books), which was short-listed for Binghamton University's Milt Kessler Poetry Book Award, and *Paper Birds Don't Fly,* released in April 2016 by New York Quarterly Books. Al has served on the Board of Directors of The Writers Place, The Brick Mountain Foundation, The Little Balkans Press, and currently sits on the board of Woodley Press at Washburn University in Topeka. He regularly drank coffee at the White Buffalo Café and Emporium and was once photographed eating the largest baloney sandwich ever served at 7th and Broadway.

Acknowledgments from the Author

These poems were previously published in *The Last Hippie of Camp 50* (Woodley Press), *Finding the Edge* (Woodley Press), *Cooking Chili on the Day of the Dead* (Aldrich Press), *Waving Mustard in Surrender* (NYQ Books). I wish to thank the editors for supporting writers like myself. I'd like to give a nod to the poets—Adam Jameson, J.T. Knoll, and Melissa Fite Johnson—with whom I share these pages; to Robert Stewart, William Trowbridge, and Jo McDougall for their advice on this thematic collection of previously collected poems; and then, of course, to the editors at Spartan Press and 39 West Press, especially Jason Ryberg, Jeanette Powers, and Will Leathem. As of this first printing, the rumors of Michael Hogard's death are unsubstantiated, but the wake is ongoing.

BACKYARD UNIVERSE

MELISSA FITE JOHNSON

*In memory of Knuckles,
the beloved dog in these poems*

Summer Wedding

Midwestern Bride advised drying
my bridal bouquet—tying the stems
to a hanger and letting
the sunflower heads dangle.

But I couldn't watch
vibrant colors drain like blood
from the face of a dying man.
I couldn't intentionally harden
each petal into crumble
at the slightest touch. Instead,

I parked my car across the street from
my father's grave and sidestepped
the 5:00 traffic. I said nothing and left
my flowers to dry under the Kansas sun.

Ode to a Mason Jar

MaMa didn't own any Tupperware.
She lined our trunk with rows of Mason jars
from her pantry shelves—quarts of canned
apricots and applesauce, carrots and beans.
I loved the care she took in preparing her jars—
quilting scraps tucked under the lids
so they'd swoosh over the lip of each jar
like a bed skirt. Even now when I buy
farmer's market jam, absentmindedly trace
the raised lettering of a cursive *B-a-l-l*,
the gesture takes me to my grandmother's pantry.

At home we drank not from iced tea glasses,
fancy with their frosted horizontal stripes,
but from simple Mason jars—pints of orange
juice before school, tap water at dinner.
Fridays were special. We ordered pizza,
rented a movie, were allowed one glass of pop.
Even now when I visit Mom for dinner
and could swig the moonshine that most belongs
in this jar, I choose pop. I savor that Friday
privilege in both hands, swaying slightly to hear
the faint music of ice cubes clinking against glass.

When Marc and I married, we didn't want
red roses in crystal vases. On each table were
the Mason jars of my childhood—most colorless,
but a few the light blue of a Tiffany jewelry box.
Certainly they felt just as special,
filled not with MaMa's blackbean salsa
or forbidden dark cola but with explosions of color—
sunflowers, red berries, purple statis, white daisies.

Scattered around our simple centerpieces
were jelly jars of candlelight that echoed
against glass and under the faces of our loved ones.

1931
for MaMa and PaPa

When he said, *Be my wife*,
she thought about it, being his wife,
collecting eggs and walking miles
to sell them, loosening
his children from her body, dying
in the same town where she was born.
She'd convey brilliance
through Scrabble games, not college,
though her children would go.
He'd work too hard, die
thirteen years before she did, and her last days
would be whittled away
in a nursing home. At nineteen,
she could picture this future, this little life,
and she took his hand, walked with him
to the justice of the peace
during halftime of a school ballgame.

Snapshot

A friend came over last month to take
family pictures: my husband, me, the dog,
four chickens. This photo's just Marc and me,
my favorite. I'm grinning like a kid,
my head on his shoulder, my arms linking one of his,
his face scrunched up against
my fuzzy hat, his hand on my knee.
We're sitting on the front porch of our first home
in Kansas, casually-on-purpose showcasing
new siding and paint. DayGlo yellow is *out*
this year, sophisticated gray *in*. Clearly
grown-ups live here. Both teachers
in our early thirties, we finally fit that description.
Marc's jacket and flannel shirt suggest 90s grunge,
my long straight hair the sixties. I like that
we can't be pinned down. Grandchildren
would puzzle over this picture,
try to determine when it was taken.
Maybe Marc and I won't even remember for sure—
When did we redecorate? Marc, when did you
grow that beard? Melissa, when did you
buy that coat? Our years together will blend
into a crazy patchwork quilt—impossible to
distinguish one square from the rest.

A Postcard to My Husband in Kansas

I write "Love ya" instead of
"In times of separation, I realize
reasons I love you, ones so small
they usually slip through
cracks in my mind. For example, the way
you call your headlamp a *chicken light*,
fastening it like a bandana
before sliding open the screen door
and swinging crazily at a mess of bugs
on your way to the coop."

I write "Miss you both!"
the exclamation point light and airy
instead of "My heart breaks
being away from the dog. Is he
on hunger strike because I'm away?
Does he think I've died?
Please explain I haven't,
even though I explained that myself
before I left. When I call, will you
hold the phone under his floppy ear?"

I write "Beach was great"
because I don't want the mail carrier
to know my neuroses
have followed me to California,
that while I enjoyed reading
a whole book on a towel, now my
computer is open to a scroll of
sunstroke symptoms, a cold water bottle
pressed as dramatically to my forehead
as the back of my hand could be.

Window Seat Haiku

Rip the flat building
from the ground, drink from it like
a flask of bourbon.

Dip a quill into
the dark lake, scroll a letter
down an open field.

Scatter breadcrumbs in
the cemetery, leave a
trail of bronzed headstones.

Song for Kansas

The musician calls storms the best
melodies: wind rattles its chorus
against shutters, raindrops echo
a refrain down the chimney.

The lyricist calls wheat fields
the best words: bleached stalks
wave to the muted sky. A bird flies,
left to right, like eyes over a page.

After the Beep

With her keyboard, she found a tune
so we could sing our message,
as if we were a giddy couple
corny from having finished the nursery
instead of roommates creating a summer Sunday.

We pressed *record* a dozen times
before it all came together: her music, our lyrics—

> *we were home sometimes*
> *but not all the time*
> *this was one of those times*

—the laughter we wouldn't keep to ourselves.

High School Pep Band

My flute part never sounded like the song
on its own. When I practiced,
my brother poked his head in my room,
asked if I had any idea what the hell I was doing.
But with the band, the flutes' voices soared
higher than the trumpets' bold balloon squeaks.

The trumpets—and indeed the trombones,
saxes, tubas, even clarinets—
none of them questioned our worth.
We had each other's backs. We had to.

At basketball games, we held a kind of
nerd power. No one said much
to us in classes or the halls, but they
loved us at games. They yelled
the words to every song. Together we
lifted those boys, high as the cheerleaders
somersaulting into the air. We were
part of something on those nights.
We were really in high school.

On Mondays we were back to visitor status,
stepping aside to let a row of letter jackets pass.

Olive Street House Concerts, Pittsburg, Kansas

Dinner first. In this small kitchen,
everyone becomes friends quickly. We
brush shoulders as we make our way
to the patio and back to the potluck.
Sometimes the stranger we strike up with
turns out to be the musician
in the makeshift concert hall—a living room
missing its coffee table and couch, lined
instead with chairs. Years ago, Rob built
a stage where most would put a TV.
Carol hung twinkle lights and
fastened a spotlight to the chandelier.

Then the concert, a few hours
with nomads from Austin, the Ozarks,
Scranton. They play guitar, upright bass,
harmonica. They play the fiddle and banjo.
Their voices are clear and strong:

This one's for my niece,
in too big a hurry to grow up.
This one's about my haunted apartment.
This one's for the man
I thought I'd marry but didn't.
This one's about the VW van I took
on tour that broke down twelve times.

Listening, we could feel boring
for having become teachers. Why didn't we
learn guitar, get over stage fright
by performing to a crowd of Cabbage Patch kids?

We should've marked up maps with stars
for every place we ever wanted to go,
plotted tours by connecting all those dots.

Or—and this is what I recommend—
we can just feel happy
to have found this private clubhouse,
where the password is $12
and coffee cake or calamari. We can feel
happy for food in our bellies and songs
in our ears, happy Rob and Carol have
opened their home. Happy that
in these nights, we become another story to tell.

For the Girl at Kauffman Stadium

She fashions a fluff of cotton candy
into a mustache, slurps the last from her
souvenir cup. Her whole body jitters.
She holds her homemade sign
crooked over her head, tells her
grandmother what to chant on the count
of three. No, she doesn't need anyone
to go with her to the bathroom.
Opening her mouth wide, she points
to what next month's braces will fix.

For the Woman at The Mall Deli

If she'd wanted to eat dinner alone,
she would've baked a spinach quiche.

He should have called the minute
he knew he'd be late. She did not
come here to read or work a crossword.
This is more humiliating than the time
Penny met her for Easter services
in an above-knee skirt and no hat.

She makes a show of eye-rolling
and sighing. Her husband
had better be having a heart attack.
She beckons the waitress for the time,
though she's facing the wall clock.

She splits the head off a sugar packet,
contemplates walking out.

Across the deli, a man in a blue work shirt
thinks she looks like his dead wife,
except for the eyes. He orders
a refill and a second slice of apple pie.

Walking Alone on North Broadway

I round the corner in shorts
and a tank. The town drives by.
I don't tug the hem of my shirt,
place a flat hand on my soft stomach.
I don't hear honks or whistles,

only birds calling to one another,
their incredible bodies lifting them
into the blue sky,
the way my childhood
trampoline once lifted mine.

Poetry Group

In the first weeks of short sleeves,
we move from the dining room
to the screened-in porch. Something about
sipping hot tea, feasting on homemade muffins,
listening to birds chatter
and feeling a breeze on my arms

makes everyone's poems better. Or maybe
we just aren't critical out here in the sunshine.
Today, I am a good writer,
with infinite poems ahead of and behind me.

Watching My Husband Cook

He moves down the length of the counter,
a pianist scooting left on the bench
to play the lower notes,
three steady notches
in the cutting board. A bag rustles.
The fridge door opens and shuts.

I offer to help. He answers no.
He's the cook. I sit in the living room,
write the poetry—
which is pretty and all,
but we wouldn't starve without it.

He caps a turret of steam
with the pot's lid. He pours water
and elicits the magician's puff of smoke.

Ode to Washing Dishes

First, make sure your sink is under a window.
Look outside while you fill the basin. If daytime,
don't scrutinize your lawn. Do laugh
at quarreling birds or your own yawning dog.
If night, be kind to your reflection.
Appreciate your long arms that disappear
at the wrists and the wrinkles at your mouth.

Don't think of this task as another in a hundred.
It is the reward when those are done,
the chocolate mousse after steamed vegetables.
If the hot water and bubbles,
the lavender smell, the wine glass
to your left and soft terrycloth
against your bare shoulder are not a comfort
in this late hour, then you are doing it all wrong.

Good Housekeeping

I.
The mother of my childhood
is propped up by the vacuum handle.
Her arms disappear at the ends
into filmy sink water.
She scrubs the kitchen floor the hard way,
sponge instead of mop. She's tired.

She won't stop
my father's cancer from sweeping
through our tidy lives,
but she is armed
with spray bottles and paper towels.

II.
My father's smoking
transformed the bathroom vent
from flute smooth to caked fireplace ash.
I pictured his lungs changing texture,
his heart no longer a red flame
but the doused black matchstick.

I tried hiding his cigarettes.
He always found them. Eventually,
I learned the joy my mother took in controlling
what could be. I polished the vent
with a pretty white cloth,
tenderly as she did her collection of tea spoons.

No One Could Agree Where to Bury Dad

His sister wanted him in his hometown,
Dadeville, Missouri, where he sank baskets
and wrote editorials for the school paper.
One of the first Peace Corps celebrities,
he chain-smoked nervously, drank
to fit the extroverted ideal. He squirmed
when interviewed. Handsome like Redford,
he forever had a mic under his chin.

My mom wanted him in my hometown,
Pittsburg, Kansas, where he spent
his last years, where his legend unraveled.
The laryngectomy left him with a whisper.
After the strokes he leaned into his cane,
dragged his paralyzed right half
behind his not-strong-but-stronger left.
The heart attack took him down for good.

My mom and aunt let me, then sixteen,
make the choice. Solomon's solution—cut
the baby in half—appealed only to the woman
who didn't love enough to be selfless.
But the opposite feels true in this case,
when everyone agreed to halving his ashes.
It's nice having my father so close, in the town
where I grew up and he stopped.
Nice, too, for the town that raised him
and set him free to have him back at last.

Elegy for Three Local Businessmen

Gently, my dermatologist raised my chin
to his gaze. His expression neutral, he swiveled
my head left, then right. In seventh grade,
I relished these appointments,
someone's hands on my ruined face.

The day before he died, Dennis
at the full service station shut my hood,
patted it twice. *Now you know as much
about cars as I do,* he said with a wink.
I drove off, glad that didn't have to be true.

The ceramicist once asked me to write
a poem for his wife. I imagined he sculpted
every other block of clay into a gift for her.
Where will we put this one? she'd ask, smiling,
hands in the air. Another bowl on the mantel.

Linger

I never want to leave where I am
even if where I am is the dentist's office.
I get all cozy on the soft couch with a magazine
waiting to sign insurance papers,
and nothing else matters.

Once I get to, say, the video store
I won't want to leave there either,

even though after the video store
is home: my husband, dinner made, our dog's
breath on my hand, backyard chickens
bobbing rotten apples beyond the kitchen window,
a good book, another couch.

Even when that waits, I'm content
to spend hours winding lazy figure 8s through aisles,
reading: Alaskan wilderness, five students
with nothing in common, Woodsboro murders,
meet-cute on a train in Austria.

Lazy Sonnet

Rain falls, branches droop
from the weight of
mulberries. One chicken,
framed in the open door
of the coop like the bird
inside a cuckoo clock,
bellows from her perch.
The dog refuses to go out
in the wet. He stays
with me, next to the open
sliding door, both of us
sprawled on the wood floor
like indoor campers,
my head on his soft belly.

Sonnet for Rain

After the rain passes,
the town is glad,
stirring water from umbrellas
and drawing them closed.

One little girl is sad
to see it end. She bounds
up to a tree so young
she can touch her thumbs

and fingertips around its trunk,
which she shakes, laughing,
until drops un-cling
from leaves on the boughs

and she is standing
under her own happy rain cloud.

For Our Backyard Tree

I noticed the Bartlett pear tree
through the kitchen window during
an open house. I imagined
washing dishes while gazing at blossoms
in May, a busy tire swing in five years.

The tree waited for us to move in
before shedding limbs after lightning storms.
We become efficient at clean-up—
bend our backs to become
human wheelbarrows, make tracks in soft
grass as we drag branches behind us.

The tree is dying. Only a third remains.
The top leaves form a sharp diagonal line,
a cut-out against the sky in the shape of a see-saw
that holds a parent on the left side,
a child feeling like king of the planet on the right.

The biggest crevice isn't tucked away
facing the fence. I stare into it
each time I bring my tea onto the porch
to watch sparrows tightrope a surviving branch.
When I daydream out the window
or keep my husband company while he grills
on the patio, I imagine the tree gone.
I'm glad it made itself beautiful
long enough to entice us into our home,
sorry it can't keep the act going.

Fire Pit

After the lightning storms, our backyard
tree became a scooped-out hole.
Our chickens peck near the roots that still
stretch through dark soil. My husband
chopped branches into firewood,
the trunk into uneven seats. We toast
marshmallows in memory, give thanks.

Pecan Picking
   for Glenda

Everything on the ground is the color
of tree bark. My earth-coated fingertips
are my eyes, sifting through cracked leaves,
pausing at every smooth pecan.

Even while sprawled on a picnic blanket,
my spine arched like a seal's, this work feels
primitive, as if a family's survival depends
on my filling one bucket, then another.

Under the bluest sky in weeks,
my head is too busy for worries or even dreams.

Resurrecting the Garden
for Lyn

When they separated, she left
the house her husband built,
sorry to leave her garden, knowing
he'd let it go to weed. When he died
two years later, she returned.
She tried not to look at the whole
wild picture, only the semicircle
she could draw in the dirt
with her clog. For weeks she cleared
one small bit at a time, passing
June afternoons under the blue sky.
Nights were spent on her porch,
savoring her daily cigarette,
watching not weeds but darkness
overtake purple coneflowers.
She planted a magnolia tree
in her husband's ashes. Across
the garden, sunflowers bloomed.

My Grandparents at the Piano

After PaPa died, MaMa gave us grandchildren
a recording of them at the piano, not singing,
plunking out Methodist hymns. From the record's
first static-filled breath, I can picture them
younger than I am now, him on the left
lifting the heavy notes, her with closed eyes
until he goosed her in the ribs. Neither sang,
but both sometimes hummed, the loud kind
that slips out only when the mind
isn't occupied with even the smallest troubles.

At My Grandmother's Funeral

Eventually, a conversation we once had—
about whistling, how we both had a gift for it—
rises to the surface. I try to think of
our other talks, but I only see
a very old woman in a blue bathing cap
and a very young girl in floaties
whistling together in the YMCA locker room.

At My Student's Visitation

The whole town goes when it's a kid.
I'd only known him a month. As his teacher,
I was expected. The funeral home,
used to Alzheimer's patients from nursing homes,
was unprepared for us. For two hours we waited
in a bursting hallway. I collapsed
against the wall, imagining myself as
a partial ironing board tucked inside a closet.
With every breath, I felt guilty
for taking air from our diminishing supply.
For a moment, getting out of the hallway was a relief.

The coffin was in the visitation room, closed
because of the accident. His school picture was
blown up to poster size. I locked eyes with it,
him, the whole walk down the aisle,
wondering for the first time
if he'd ever been kissed. I hadn't, at his age.
When I reached his parents, I thought of
how many hands I'd shake at teacher conferences
the next week, and that thought broke me.

Outside the funeral home, the night
was clean and wet. I choked on fresh air.

Teachers' Spring Break

10:39 p.m., and we're still up.
Marc's contacts are swimming in their
saline baths, and I'm in my pj's,
but we're still up. We're reading,

not in bed, but stretched out
on opposite ends of the couch,
my feet tucked under Marc's side.
The neighbor's dog barks

his usual indignations outside
our bedroom window. Tonight
we hardly hear him over
the woman singing in our CD player.

Our sleepytime tea is steeping
in the kitchen. Soon one of us—Marc,
I hope—will journey twenty feet,
pour two mugs, and return.

Apologia for Not Wanting Children

I come home from work, collapse
my bags on the table, find you
standing over a boiling pot.
You give a low whistle
as Jarrod Dyson steals third on the radio,
then purse your lips for a kiss.
The dog gallops in, a few beats later
than he used to. We wince
as he scatterpaws over hardwood.
He shuffles, not limps, away. You exhale.

I place my wedding ring in the dish
where it clinks against yours, fill the sink.
Outside, the chickens dance the mashed potato,
dig their clawed feet in dirt. I twist
the dishwand inside a coffee mug.
When Alex Gordon hits a home run,
we rush into the living room
to watch the replay on the muted TV.

Nothing is missing.
No baby cries from a blanket
spread on the floor as if for a picnic
of bottled breast milk and dry Cheerios.
No chubby arms reach for me.
No hands open and close
like lips desperate for words.
But nothing is missing. You have
my full attention. I have yours.

Broody

I.
I can't relate to Molly the broody
virgin hen, who sits in vain
on a mound of eggs, her parched
beak mouthing a hopeless lullaby.

I've taken a pill a day
for thirteen years. If I were a chicken,
I'd burrow my body in soft dust,
then flap grains from my feathers
as I flew, majestic ruler over the backyard
universe a few feet below.

II.
Last week I pried open
the coop door to retrieve eggs,
instead found Molly, our biggest
black hen, glowering on her nest.

She's been there since, refusing to
leave her eggs, panting
in her sweatbox, making herself ill,
her comb tinged purple from dehydration.

To break her of her broodiness,
my husband slid an ice pack beneath her
damp haunches; I tried
baptizing her head in a bowl of water.

We locked Molly outside her coop
with food and water, rolled up the tractor.
She paced the length of the cage,
desperate to return to her nest.

III.
We've stopped worrying Molly will die
now that she's worked out a plan with
the other chickens. One covers her shift
on the nest long enough for
Molly to stretch her legs,
take a long sip at the waterer.

But now there's the issue of no rooster.
Those eggs might as well be ping-pong balls;
they're not hatching, no matter
how long Molly or a stand-in squat over them.

IV.
I can't relate to Molly the broody
virgin hen, who sits in vain
on a mound of eggs, her parched
beak mouthing a hopeless lullaby,

but I'll support her choice,
ask a neighbor for a fertilized dozen,
help lift my determined hen's body
up and over them, do what I can
for her to become a mother.

Visiting the Dead

If I squint hard against the sun,
I can make out a crooked door
cut into the sky. For an hour or two,
I'd like to leave this familiar place,

enter a world of blue-tinged light
emanating from an old television.
I'd flip to *Wheel of Fortune,*
sit beside my father on his couch,

try to guess the phrases before he does.
During commercials, I'd show him
photos of my husband, laugh when Dad
scrunches his face in mock disapproval.

I'd touch his Adam's apple—
new, plugging the hole cancer made—
hear his gravelly voice for the first time.
Eventually, I'd smooth my skirt,

kiss Dad's cheek, find myself again
barefoot in a world of green,
my backyard, where Marc would
slide open the screen door to join me.

MELISSA FITE JOHNSON

In 1984, the same year the White Buffalo Café and Emporium closed its doors, three-year-old Melissa Fite Johnson moved to Pittsburg, KS. She never left. The town fostered in her a love of literature and writing. She earned a Master's Degree in English Literature from Pittsburg State University and currently teaches English at her alma mater, Pittsburg High School. Her poems have appeared in *Valparaiso Poetry Review*, *Broadsided Press*, *Midwest Quarterly*, *Red Paint Hill Journal*, and elsewhere, and her first collection, *While the Kettle's On* (Little Balkans Press, 2015), won the Nelson Poetry Book Award and is a Kansas Notable Book. Melissa and her husband, Marc, live in Pittsburg with their four backyard chickens. Connect with her online at melissafitejohnson.com.

Acknowledgments from the Author

I'm so honored to be part of the rich tradition of Little Balkans writers and happy to be included in this love letter to Southeast Kansas, my home since I was a child. A special thanks to Al Ortolani, J.T. Knoll, Adam Jameson, and the editors at Spartan Press and 39 West Press. Sincere gratitude to the editors who first published the poems in this book—some originally appeared in *While the Kettle's On* (Little Balkans Press); others, in *Bear Review*, *Cave Region Review*, *I-70 Review*, *The KLC Journal*, *Quatrain. Fish*, *Red Eft Review*, *Rust + Moth*, and *velvet-tail*. Many thanks to the members of my beloved workshop group: Laura Lee Washburn, Allison Blevins, Chris Anderson, and Roland Sodowsky. Finally, I'd like to thank my incredibly supportive friends and family, especially Emmy and David Fite, Glenda Madl, Donna Johnson, and, as always, Marc Johnson, who is the best person I ever could've gotten mixed up with.

SMALL TOWN

ADAM JAMESON

*This book is for my grandfathers,
David C. Jameson and Robert M. Bowers*

Wild Red Berry Field

Piccini on the mound,
Jameson behind the plate.

They are 12.
I'm letting them call their own game.

I was this way 30 years ago.

The count is 1 and 2.
Runner on 2nd.

2 dads sitting on buckets
in the dugout door watch
a change-up spin toward
home plate.

Jameson squeezes the foul tip
as Piccini pumps his fist.

Splitting Wood on Robert Bly's Birthday

First day of my winter vacation.
Bored by 9:30 I headed for the
shop and Grandpa's wedge
maul and ax.

Mrs. Mitchell's son had cut
down a big ash in the fall.
Russian and I had cut it up
after 6 weeks of no-show
from the son.

It was still piled on my back
property line.
I didn't need the wood.

Already had 4 cords stacked
under the pines to the north.
What I did need was some
silence.
Splitting wood by hand tends
to keep the people away.

I split till twilight.
The only sounds were me
cussing under my breath
and the sharp rap of Grandpa's
maul hitting the wedge.

Watering the Oaks

Twilight on Sunday evening.
Yoger's cutting wheat on the
80 across the road.

He throws me a quick wave
from the cab before spinning
the combine to make another pass.
I used to take him chunks of
flathead every October.

I don't have time to get
to the river anymore.
He has to make do with
crappie in April.

Cole and I are working
on his change-up.
Scooter is asleep in the grass.

It has been dry of late and my wife
is watering 3 towering oaks on the
west side of the house.

I don't dare tell her my uncle
planted those oaks in 1953
and don't need watered.

I crouch for one more change-up
and watch her water the oaks anyway.

Southpaw Catcher

At the tryouts the coach told me
that no left-hander would
ever play catcher for him.

I just shrugged my shoulders
and walked back to sit
with the rest of the parents.

2 games in and 17 passed
balls later, he finally let
Cole put the gear on.

We were on our 4th pitcher.
My wife glanced at me
when she heard the click

of the pitch counter.
We got run-ruled in 4 innings.
I waited till everyone had left.

I showed the coach the counter.
It read 28, the number of pitches
in the dirt that game.

I made an O with my fingers and
told him that was how many went
to the backstop. I had a 12-year-old

left-hander with a fat lip, 2 deep
bruises and a missing fingernail,
laughing at his
dirty face in the truck mirror.

Friday Night Lights

It had been 24 years since I'd been
on Hutch field under the lights.
My son was going to be the ball boy.

We got there early and as he hustled
balls around during the pre-game warm up,
I sat on the bench alone,
thinking it felt good to be home.
The storm we'd been watching all
day appeared, and they hustled
us off the field and into the old
south locker room.

The same locker room I played in
as a kid back in the 70s while my dad,
Kabance, Wilson and Bournoville
watched whirring film of that
week's foe.
If I was a good boy while the men
worked, I'd get a Pepsi out of
the fridge at the end of the night.

While we waited, the coach
talked as we watched a little film.
Standing by the door, I could see
Cole sitting in the middle of the
team, not moving, studying the
film like all the rest.

The first play from scrimmage
was a toss sweep to the Barnes kid.

He turned the corner in
front of us and was off down
the sideline.

I turned to look for Cole.
He was already gone, down
the sideline, chasing the play.
I started to walk toward the
end zone but stopped.

At some point a father has
to start letting his boy become
a man, and I figured there
was no better time and place.

Saturday

Sitting in the sunshine of
Saturday afternoon drinking
beer and writing.

My son riding his bike with
the other kids all over
the campground.

Scooter the Shitzu asleep in the sun.
Wife reading a book in the lounge chair.
Trees in half bloom. Crappie biting.

Camper windows open, letting
the Kansas spring flow through and
cover our pillows.

The deer sneak up at dusk to
eat acorns just outside the firelight.

Only I can see them, everyone else
is busy talking about nothing.

I say a monk prayer of gratitude
between bites of crappie and sips of beer
as the bull bats sweep low over the water,
gathering their supper in silence.

Summer

I've mowed and weed-whacked an acre.
Cut up the top of an old elm that
blew down in the storm last week.

Took my son and nieces to town
for ice cream.

Checked the tomato plants
and gave the neighbor's dog
a treat or two.

It's twilight.
I'm sitting on the deck, drinking
my supper again and watching
the wrens bed down in the
birdhouse to the west.

Beaver Lake

Twilight at the lake.
Cole goes for one last bike ride.

The Jacksons retired yesterday.
This is their 1st trip with
the camper and boat.

I help him back it down the ramp
and quietly ask God to bless
them as they head out in search
of channel cat.

I'm back in my chair.
Cold beer in my hand,
watching fireflies turn
circles just outside the firelight.

Night before the Series

I'm on the deck, listening
to the radio replay of Game 7 from 1985.

Grandpa never missed a game.
He could be found on the
breezeway of his house over
in East Town whenever the
Royals were on.

Grandkid's birthdays, Easter,
wedding anniversaries, you
name it, all had to be planned
around the Royals on radio.

In spring it was work pants
and a jacket, summer was the same
work pants and undershirt, fall
was back to the jacket.
It was my job to sit quietly on
the chaise lounge and fetch
Budweiser from the fridge.

If the game ran late or the weather
was bad, Grandma would stick her
head out the door.
He would dismiss her with a
grunt and wave of his hand.

It's where I heard Denny Matthews
talk about the speed of Wilson, the
slick fielding of White, Brett with another
double off the wall, and the Quis

coming to slam the door in the 9th.
I'm 43 and I can still see them in my
mind all these years later.

So when this run started with the
wildcard game against the A's,
I turned off the TV and took my
son out on the deck to listen
on the radio.

When it got late, my wife
stuck her head out the door
and saw me sitting there with
a cold Bud and a 12-year-old
sound asleep in the lawn chair.

Lincoln Park

Runner on 2nd.
The batter hits one
to center.

I see the 3rd base coach
wind-milling his arm ... he's
sending the runner
home.

I glance at Cole.
He's up, mask off, ready for the throw.

Trey, our center fielder, has a
million-dollar arm.

It's going to be a close play.
Parents from both sides
are yelling.
I'm silently sitting on my bucket
in the dugout door.

Ball arrives on perfect short hop,
through the dust I can see Cole
sliding to deliver a shin guard
sandwich.

Dylan, the young ump,
former catcher, punches
the runner out with a
resounding, *Got 'em!*

Parents are still yelling.

My assistant coaches are hooting
and hollering.
The other coach is mad about
us blocking the plate.

I'm still on my bucket, silent.
It's the 1st out of the 1st inning.

Cole winks at me and throws
the ball back to the pitcher.

Fall Day

Got up before dawn
and made coffee in the
dark kitchen.
My phone vibrated
and buzzed.

Email ... we had trouble
on Mulberry 23-4 last
night.
I shut it off and stuck it
in the drawer by
the coffee pot.

On the deck, the eastern sky
pinkish and purple, I see
Mr. Socks the cat nosing
around in my garden.
A doe and fawn eating acorns
in Mrs. Mitchell's yard.

3 teal buzz overhead, make
a hard right and land
on Stefanoni's pond.
Mr. Russian shuffles out
his driveway to get his paper.

I spent the week taking care
of linemen, troubleshooters,
mechanics, designers and
supervisors from Pittsburg
to Wichita.

I really should take a look
at the Mulberry circuit, but
I'm going to rake leaves, cut
wood and leave that phone
in the drawer till Monday.

Frank Ferraro

After a game he used to
pile Denny and me in the
back seat of his Cadillac.

Covered in dirt and chalk,
we'd sink deep into the leather
and let the AC cool our sweat.

He and Dee would talk over
the game with us as we cruised
south, headed for cokes and burgers.

Denny and I would order a
couple of cheeseburgers and fries.

Frank would open his wallet
with his thick plumber
fingers, fish in among
the hundreds and come out
with a 20.

He'd always tell the girl
behind the counter to get
us another burger or 2.
These are growing boys.

After a hard-fought victory
this summer, I took my
team to the snow cone stand.

Two of my favorites asked
for a 2nd cone. Smiling, I handed
the girl a 20 and said better
get these boys a couple of more.

Wind Storm

I found Underwood and the crew
12 miles west of Humboldt
just after 2 a.m.

I brought them a transformer
and 3 pizzas.

We ate by headlight
in the middle of the road.
Wind singing through the weeds.

bottle rockets

walking with dogs
and pear trees
in bloom reminded me
of mom canning
pickles with Carol Rink

as a kid, content
with my zebco 33,
johnny hardcranker,
minnows and cork,
channel cats at dusk,
crappie in the spring
with grandma and her
cane pole, the arc
of her casts, the girlish
giggle as she landed
keeper after keeper,

Johnny Marietta at
the corner store, eating
frito pies and telling
lies, me buying
illegal bottle rockets
from Johnny's wife Helen
at the fireworks stand
in the back of the store

Waylon and Willie
were kings
dad's construction crew
drinking beer out back
of the shop

late on friday nights,
me sneaking sips as they
slipped out to piss in the weeds,

walking Bobby Brooks home drunk
so Norma could yell at him
as he opened the front door,

Old Sam and Bertha Brown,
chickens and cows
across the road,

me racing to their house
on halloween, special
cupcakes on the table,

stray dog after stray dog
dropped off in our driveway,
rocky penny groana tequila fritz
and all the rest unnamed
flood my brain every time
I see a dog

shrink away from me today,

walking with dogs
and pear trees
in bloom, as close to heaven
as I ever need to be

Baseball Below the Light
for Uncle Trout and Father Two Beavers

I sit on my porch at sunset
hearing Number 11 go south
across Quincy, mixed with
the rhythmic thump thump
of the kid across the street,
dribbling left and hitting
a fade away jumper in the twilight.

I remember eating sanchos
in a roadside taco stand
20 miles north of Santa Fe
with Uncle Trout.
Me—18-year-old college freshman,
Uncle Trout—old and wise, giggling
his marijuana laugh between bites
of bean and tortilla
as I tried to explain my black eye.

I think of Father Two Beavers
over on Euclid—the wind rising
and tossing cottonwood leaves
across the driveway.
I can hear the crunch of a middle linebacker
smacking heads with a tailback
on Friday night, and I know
I will never be that alive again.
Darkness comes and I listen to the Royals
on my grandfather's radio—remembering
his smell of dust, sweat, and coffee
at the end of the work day.

The streetlight blinks on, and within minutes
a small team of boys appear
for a game of baseball below the light.

My porch is a ground-rule double.
I smile when Jake smacks one to within
inches of my chair. The boys
need a pitcher with a curve.
They send the runt over to inquire
about my arm.

I am reminded of Uncle Trout
and Father Two Beavers
playing ball in the light
above the Frontenac Cemetery,
and the back door slider
my dad taught me to throw.

Routine

On Saturdays in the fall I'll unplug my
phone and do nothing more than sit
on the porch all day long without moving my chair.
Maybe put on a Tommy Dorsey or Glenn Miller
record and let her nap on the couch in the gray
flannel shirt I bought her for Christmas.

I walk to the corner store to eat frito pies
with the asphalt boys and dump truck drivers.
They are my kind of people—dirty jeans, hands
calloused and covered with nicks and cuts
from work, open to the wind.

My neighbor usually wanders over to talk about
crabgrass or the weather or bagworms.
I just nod my head as if I really care and wonder
how the Royals managed to blow
a 4-run lead the night before.

The call of my pet hoot owl signals the onset of darkness.
I pull on a ragged sweatshirt to ward off the coolness of
October and fire up the grill to cook thick steaks,
a romantic dinner complete with full moon and the rumble
of a coal train headed south out of Pittsburg.

She emerges from the house with a cold beer for me
and a glass of wine for her—from the west comes
the sound of a coyote, smiling at the thought
of the leftovers I always leave for him under
the willow in the backyard.

I Always Take the Call

The sleet has been coming down
for hours now.

I've been lying awake in bed
listening to it pepper
the window.

The wind gusts, and off to
the east, down by Cow Creek,
I hear the crack and crash of tree
top falling to earth.

I roll a little closer to her warmth.

To the south, by the old Pogson
farm a coyote throws his voice
into the wind.

Immediately from the west comes
his answer.

I wonder what they are saying
to one another on a night
like this and wish I spoke coyote.

My cell phone vibrates on the
night stand.

It's the service operator in Topeka.
We've got a small outage north
of McCune and the line crew
needs a ground man.

Before I roll out of bed I kiss
her on the ear for good luck and
dress in the dark listening
to the coyotes sing.

Twilight

The smell of my juniper
logs in the charcoal
pit make me long to be on the
road again—out in the desert
under a full moon—or on a
little two-lane hi-way in
eastern Mississippi, dotted
with tar paper shacks and
roadhouses filled with big
orders of greasy ribs and
full-breasted southern
waitresses.
Darkness in Kansas never falls—it
glides from east to west
in slow motion—leaving me
time to finish my steaks and
decide where it is that I want
my words to take me.

Wading the River

When the whites get to running,
people line the bank shoulder
to shoulder.

I figured out how to wade the
moving water to escape
the crowd. Learned

to shuffle my feet
along the bottom, probing
for the deep holes that

meant drowning. Learned
how to read the water
and spot an eddy the size of

a baseball where the really
big ones went to feed.
Egyptian History let out at

12:30 and by 1:30 I was at
the Baxter Springs dam with
at least 5 keepers on the stringer.

I was the toast of the river
that spring. I even had my picture
on the front page of the *Joplin Globe*.

The caption called me
a *Sportsman*. Hell, I still don't know
what a sportsman is. I didn't dare

tell the reporter I was a mostly
broke college kid
who just liked to wade the river.

It was my personal form of therapy.
Mom got sick that fall, and I never
got back to the river

until the day my 8-year-old
wanted to learn to wade.
Secretly, I wanted to see if I still

had the touch. My son
doesn't know anything about therapy,
and he never got to know

his grandma Sheryl.
What he does know
is how to wade the river

and catch white bass.

Snow Geese

Frogs croaking in the ditch remind me
this gravel road is close enough to
heaven for me.
South wind up from Texas—carrying Kiowa
and Comanche songs—rocks my empty hammock.

Rain comes and goes quietly at dawn.
The lead switchman on 23rd Street
curses himself for forgetting his rain suit.
Grandma's '68 Ford Galaxy, strong
Detroit steel, knocks, pings, shudders
from the haul-ass drive I made earlier.

My Lab barks three times from the backyard.
He is looking for supper. I smile,
remembering the first pheasant he tried to corner
in a snow-filled Kansas ditch.

I sit on my porch, writing grilled-cheese poetry,
while high above, northbound snow geese
honk and squawk for the first time in years.

Lonestar Supper

The sun setting over the cut
wheat field filled my backyard
with innocence the color
of Neil Young's guitar.
I sat, grilling steaks, my mind
wandering over the
desolation that creeps into
a young man's head when he
is all too aware of himself.

I fingered my Jack
Kerouac postcard
and wondered if he wasn't
here, dancing a fandango
a 1/4 inch above the wet
concrete I had just finished
pouring.

Joe Azember, my old neighbor,
wanders over to share a beer
and some memories from his
days as a soldier on the beaches
in France.

All he really wants is to get
out of the house and away from
his wife, but soon her voice
can be heard floating over the
fence, calling him home so she
doesn't have to watch *Wheel
of Fortune* alone.

I watch him until he disappears
behind the giant elm tree between
our homes and reach for the
whiskey bottle on the step
next to me.

ADAM JAMESON

Adam Jameson was born and raised in Pittsburg, Kansas. He is a 1995 graduate of Pittsburg State University, where he earned a B.A. in History. His Whitmanesque job history includes self-employed construction, UPS, and Kansas City Southern Railroad. He currently works as an estimator for Westar Energy. Adam started writing poetry in high school and has spent the last 25 years performing with White Buffalo Poetry and Blues. His poems have appeared in *Harp*, *The Little Balkans Review*, and *To the Stars through Difficulty*, and his first collection of poetry, *#9 to Sallisaw*, was released in 2013 by Little Balkans Press. Adam lives in rural Pittsburg with his wife, Meredith, and son, Cole; his favorite past times are chasing pheasants in the fields of western Kansas and catching slab crappie in the strip pits around Pittsburg.

Acknowledgments from the Author

Recently, at a work meeting, a VIP made the comment, *The strength of the Southeast Kansas Division is you all love each other like family. Your weakness is you are stubborn and fight like dogs against anything you see as unworthy or false. I guess it is a small town thing.* I think it was meant as an insult, but I took it as a compliment. The poems I've selected for this book are small town. In these poems are the people, places, and attitudes that make my small town, Pittsburg, unique. I would like to tip my hat to the poets—Al *Pug* Ortolani, J.T. *Father Two Beavers* Knoll, and Melissa *Blonde Buffalo* Fite Johnson—with whom I share these pages: fine poets, without a doubt, but better people. A special thanks to the editors at Spartan Press and 39 West Press; Will Leathem, who has the best bookstore in the world; and Jason Ryberg, whose work and intelligence I admire.

OTHERS LIKE US

J.T. KNOLL

for my brothers and sisters

Grandma's Smile

Too far from freckle season
I slide between the frozen doors
into a porch swing world
where Grandma hovers for a moment
just above the gladiolas

smiling sweetly
as she remembers

the first time she jumped off.

Quilting

She gathers her sewing basket
and drives the old Ford up to the bungalow
to quilt.

Sitting around the frame
she trades the local news
and drifts back to when she had a man
and children tugged at her apron.

The air hangs fragrant as she leans over her art.

* * *

Oh the names the quilts have!

Lover's Link, Flower Garden, Bowtie and Friendship
Water Lily, Rose, Pansy, and Tulip

The Great Circle, Ocean Waves, Goose Tracks
Road To California, American Beauty, Drunkard's Path

Pinwheel, Four Patch, Star, and Necktie
Wedding Ring, Sun Bonnet, Fruit Basket, Butterfly

* * *

And the light shines good in her bones all day long.

* * *

In the evening
she drives the hill toward home
thinks about her children
and sighs.

Death Of A Railroad Man

At Friskel's Funeral Home
the soprano sings
The Old Rugged Cross
as the switch engine rumbles
from everlasting
to
everlasting.

The smell of diesel lingers.

In the distance
a horn blasts
two longs
a short
and a long cry
deep into the clear December morning.

Uncle Bill's Place

At uncle Bill's place
out by the strip pits
our families came together
as the smell of barbeque
and honeysuckle
hung low
across the humid afternoon.

I remember
that once when I was
off from the rest
I saw a bass fly
up from the dark water
into a column of light
and turn its magnificent eye
with such a searching look
that I winced
and stood
motionless until the last circle
touched
the tangled shore.

Lightning

*I'd be pretty good if I could see ... I can't read.
I can't write. I can't sew. I can't do a shit-firin'
thing.* — Aunt Helen (Arcadia, Kansas 1979)

She gropes for it in the deepest shadow
calling out her pain so elegantly

rearranging the furniture for the last time

hungry for it
becoming more iron than anything
knowing somehow it will soon return

running with the wind
falling with the rain

inviting the spark of death.

Ballad Of Matt Knoll

He gets up in the mornin'
And goes to work each day
Comes back home in the evenin'
Doesn't have much to say
The very next day it's the same thing
The day after the same
He just keeps on workin'
Never does he complain

> Even though he's down in a coal mine
> Scufflin' on his hands and knees
> Carbide lamp his only sunshine
> A dreamin' of his sweet Marie

Lost his father in a cave-in
Brother died by his side
The very same day he had a son born
Funny how birth and death collide
Funeral was a sad goodbye
Amazing Grace they did sing
Took his baby to the church font
Stood and cried at the christening

> Next day he was down in a coal mine
> Scufflin' on his hands and knees
> Carbide lamp his only sunshine
> A dreamin' of his sweet Marie

Saturday nights he drinks a little bootleg
Circlin' 'round to the polka beat
In a local immigrant dance hall
Outside town in a field of wheat

Sunday mornin' he grabs a cane pole
Goes off to fish and be alone
On the way back he sings out an old song
In his German baritone

    Monday mornin' he's back in a coal mine
    Scufflin' on his hands and knees
    Carbide lamp his only sunshine
    A dreamin' of his sweet Marie

Digging

I hear the clean, rhythmic sound of his sharpshooter — sixteen-inch blade, ash and steel handle — easing down into clay, his straining back in a deep hole, descending to a sewer line or water main. Or out back in the garden with a long-handled shovel, stooping and standing in rhythm; boot on steel, wood on knee, the blade sliding in, arms levering dark earth up and over. Digging.

Grandpa could handle a shovel. He consistently dug more coal in a day than any other man in any of the southeast Kansas mines he worked. And following that, he dug graves for horses, footings for buildings, troughs for water, sewer and gas lines, gardens for Grandma. And deep ditches in search of broken sewer pipe; heaving sod and clay and rock to one side — or over his shoulder — going down, down, and down. Digging.

How he smiled and whistled between his teeth when digging narrow trenches for new gas lines near our house — happy to be standing and shoveling above ground in clean air and sunshine rather than on hands and knees, 150 feet down, in foul, dark air, picking and shoveling coal from a 3-foot seam. And the easy, confident way he carried his tools — long-handled shovel, sharpshooter, pick, and double-bladed ax — from the bed of his pickup to the plumb line and set about his work. Digging.

The moist smell of new earth, the rasp and thump of clay, the slice of edge through roots. The economy of motion. Sewer line, water line, gas line, grave, garden, ditch. Digging.

Coal Miner Man

I go to work every day in a hole
Shovel and pick, diggin' out coal
Don't make very much. Get paid by the ton
I'm a coal miner man, a coal miner's son

I work in the dark, ride down in a cage
Try not to show how much I'm afraid
That I won't make it back to turn my face to the sun
I'm a coal miner man, a coal miner's son

> Mine owners are rich. Miners are poor
> They stand at the top. We stand at death's door
> One fall of the rock and a life's all undone
> For a coal miner man, a coal miner's son

I started at twelve. Now I'm thirty-five
That's twenty-three years I have survived
I'm proud of my work. I won't be outdone
I'm a coal miner man, a coal miner's son

I pay my dues at the union hall
And I will walk out if a strike it is called
The union has strength you can't find in just one
For a coal miner man, a coal miner's son

I toil and I save so my children can go
To school and get free — won't have to dig coal
And they will look back on how it begun
With a coal miner man, a coal miner's son

Edge Of The Pond

The goose approaches
sideways turning
into the rippled halo

testing the air on one foot.

We are the same
all flesh and feathers
at the pond's edge.

*

I reach deep into grandma
where only grandpa's hands and mine
could know the empty places
needing.

She tells me of how her father died
deep in the earth.
A miner.
Too deep.

*

Some say I could fly if I choose.
They cannot see the air in my bones
carrying me higher.

*

Her father gone
she could know nothing of men's hands
only their appetites there
in the long days beside her mother.

No wonder
she felt reborn
afraid as any baby
when he touched her there.

*

Ah now
he pulls his beak from his snowy back
and calls.
He sees from his unblinking eye
grandma flying ever nearer.

*

Riding the wings of the Bull Goose
she will cross the pond again.
I will touch the spaces
her bones leave in the air
alone.

Driving

He was in one of those periods
when there was no way to tell them
what he saw and heard.
So he traveled with his thoughts
and they thought him strange
for his anger and silence.

He wanted to tell them
how lately the spring birds
had been committing suicide
in the grill of his blue Dodge
as he drove to work.

And about the old house dog
he had seen
rolling beneath the chassis
of a tan Chevrolet
   to emerge at the tailpipe
bleeding and dazed
and make his way back to the porch.

How on Sunday afternoons
he would pass him
in his super clean '68 Biscayne
   hair in a flat-top
brother-in-law in the front
sister and mother in the back
   a space between them for dad
flickering through the countryside.

And young girls from the rear
bent in tall grass
pulling starter ropes
pulling starter ropes.

Letter To My Brothers

I am outward far from shore
trying so hard to get to you there
in the blossoming island.
I swim steadily but am blinded by snowflakes and need.
Eyes have no place to hide from this.
Blue air hangs momentarily red.
All things swirl by in search of Magellan.

In the next bedroom there sleeps a horny monk
his shoes placed neatly outward by the bed.
He dreams of the angels and beasts
who dance behind the golden door.
He is made of metal to attract lightning.

The trees beckon.
The ocean shimmers.
Farmers and sailors both with their faces in the teeth
know enough to wait.

Driving In Winter

The abundant Kansas light slanting
across the January afternoon
is not enough to lift me from a great sadness that
settled in like the ache that comes when the flu
finds you in its rounds through the winter
hallways of a school or church.
Or greets you in the eight cents change
and *Have a nice day* the clerk hands you after you
fill up the car and buy a pop and chicken tenders
that have been waiting a little too long beneath
the amber glow of the convenience store heat lamp.

Sorrow, melancholy, woe,
all are but words. Words too small to grasp this
enveloping sadness that rides inside me as we drive
— my happy-to-be-out-of-the-house father and me —
the thirty or so miles to the clinic
to get his pacemaker checked,
singing together the Sinatra songs and polka tunes
I've put on a cassette to help him forget the pain
that lives continually in his fragile heart, back and legs.

It is Monday here, Martin Luther King Jr. Day,
a thousand miles from Memphis,
where an assassin cut him down.
The grass along the roadside bleeds pale brown.
Hedge trees sculpt out a dirge.
Banks and schools and government offices are closed,
so there can be no deposits or withdrawals,
no homework given or handed in,
no papers filed, no mail delivered.

What I'm really sad about is time
and how little of it there is left.
With my dad who is moving closer,
calls me some days and says, *This is your son.*
Asks me questions like,
Where the hell did God come from?
And with my son who's moving farther away,
calls me some days and says,
Just don't worry about me, Dad,
asks me, *What God should I pray to?*

I am somewhere on the road between them,
staring intently into the glare of the highway ahead.

Sacred Heart
for brother Johnny

I remember you there on the altar
Skinny Scudzer in a waxed flat-top
wearing your cassock and surplice
   boy priest lifting the golden burner
as inapproachable light poured
thru the stained glass
below the statue of Christ
his heart opened
sacred heart burning
in your breast as you
walked a few inches above
the hardwood stage of it all
sweet sacred heart
tumbling over and over
as jazz kyries blew into the cosmos.

Or hanging in midair
as the basketball arced
toward the hoop
in the old sunken gym
sacred heart
sacred heart of the jump shot
the behind the back pass
the blur of sevens as you flicker
like a slow curve left
southpaw sacred sevens
sacred heart in the purple vortex
of Kansas twilight
I remember you.

We Will Swim Naked Again

I went last week to Whitesnake
where once we swam naked
with bass and blue gill
just like dad, Lefty,
who has his legs back
when swimming.

Oh the joy of his boy
jumping into the Y pool,
his bald pate disappearing
below the gurgle and swirl.

Took him to the E.R. next day
because of chest pain.
Mostly, though, to get
away, take a ride.
*I'm okay when I'm ridin' around
in the car with you*, he smiled
from the seat of my trendy Explorer.
In my head, I hear Ginsberg
singing father death.

Oh the entry/exit point that
we all fall toward/away from in this
brief breath of truth and suffering.

We will swim naked again, brother,
with bass and bluegill and Lefty
beneath thunderstruck southeast Kansas clouds
as Joe Speer and Jesus walk above us
on the innocent strip pit sea,
music echoing out of the timber.

Listening

Walking at 5 a.m. I listen for the dawn
in the groove of tires out on the highway.
In the park beneath the cedars
a paperboy passes through me.
Impossible to hold for long
but sweet nonetheless

and full of light.

Others Like Us
for Margie

There are others like us.
All over the world there are people
absentmindedly humming tunes
learned on AM radio.
People who hear questions
pulsating around everything
and search for others
who share this listening.

   The answer, my friend, is blowin' in the wind.
   The answer is blowin' in the wind.

It's okay. We can lie on our beds
whispering finely tuned engines of words.
And when we close our eyes,
we can walk through the world in our Keds,
which is to say,
the blessed life will always be ours.

And as the years creep upon us,
we can embrace them
like a simple twist of fate,
a twilight game of hide and seek.

   One, two, three on sixty.
   One, two, three on seventy.
   One, two, three on infinity, ha, ha.

two women in rosemary

swan
    your feathers
curtains blowing outward
from the dark window of spring
your lover climbs thru
just to see you turn your head
    blinding water watching
no shortage of void in you
no shortage of void

heart
oh heart
hung in a black steel ring
heart
queen of the vanity table drawers
no one
can open

The Riddle of Fishes
for Linda

Come
touch me in my abstract dripping
bluelove
bird singing in the dead of day
reaching wordless places
long forgotten.

Your beauty.
Why our pain?
The riddle of fishes
cut from lines of fight
only to swallow new hooks.

I love you
in the corners of paintings
where the artist ran out of
space
so much more to paint
and out of
space.

awe
    for linda

we are testing new ground now

      you in the heart chair
your legs beckoning like the planets
      and me here on the brass spaceship bed
wondering if infinity will be long enough

I remember back in '78 on wilson avenue
we rode the zephyr together

you turned to me and said
feel my breasts
it's the best thing for you
and i'm hot here
under the flaming stars

when we get to the far side of the universe
i will turn to you
and we will dance on the edge

with fear
without fear
before
and after

weeping

awed

Duet

Between the anvil and the hammer
The child waits for the pain
Trying not to shatter
Nor break the steel refrain
You say you'll take it for him
But as the arc completes
You draw back to the shadows
And view the aching meat

    You come to me with offers
    You hope I will not take
    And when I reach out for them
    You run away and say
    I've got two little children
    I don't need anymore
    When you opened up my door

On the plains above the city
The scene is set for war
Between a man and woman
The archetypal four
Not with guns or clubs or knives
Do they act out their play
But words of love and tenderness
Hang mangled in the day

And when the play is over
The props are put to rest
The audience applauding
The truth they know the best
Love is the real killer
That drops you in the hole
Where your body moves alive and well
Searching for its soul

So please don't love me baby
Please don't say sweet things
Come to me with bloody lips
And your arms bound up in rings
Of anger hate and challenge
For the innocent young boy
And tell the truth *I'll murder you
If you play too long with toys*

True Story

In my living room
a woman is outlining the steps
to insanity.
One of them is a stop at a motel.

The rains fell all through the night.
There was a wild party somewhere
and she went as an exhibitionist.

Later
her husband slammed on the gas
and she began to think she was the Virgin
— her halo a fly circle about her head.

After a week
they transferred her to lockup.
She thought this was pretty funny
for a few days

but then she began to cry
and knew
it was time to go home again.

The Mall

When life gets overwhelming
be big, oh don't be small
Just gather up your family
and go out to the mall
There's restaurants, there's clothing stores
and video arcades
You can spend up all your money
even before it's made

    At the mall, at the mall
    You can picnic with your family
    by a concrete waterfall
    At the mall, at the mall
    Where you can walk in any direction
    and always find a wall
    at your local hometown mall

The weather may get inclement, the wind it may blow
But you're safe there with your family
at a fish and boating show
And the old folks are circlin', just happy as they please
But they don't know where they're goin'
They've got old timer's disease

When you go on vacation to see what you can see
And travel over this great land so brave and free
After you've seen the parks and monuments
and you think you've seen it all
you know it's never quite complete
until you go out to the local mall

The holidays they roll around
You can't seem to get ahead
You start losin' faith in mankind
and you fear God might be dead
But you don't go to church
or temple or to the wailin' wall
You just whip out all your credit cards
and go out to the mall

Well Some People Called It Psychedelic And Others Called It 4th Of July

I awoke to the sound of plastic dancing
with the wind in a ragged hole.
The Simian just above stared to my right.
I journeyed down the long, shadowed hall
as the house dog up and rolled
into the light.
Down the back stairs quickly,
stopping only in the big barren room
to look in there for some fluorescent news
and the source of the latest boom.

Outside Tom Paine was on the corner
Standin' in a drivin' rain.
He was ragin' about and beginnin' to shout
for the madmen to be sane.
You see he knows he know he know ho hos
that we're searchin' for a king again.

I began to run out onto a concrete overpass,
lookin' for a minstrel to sing
America the Beautiful to me
at last.
Standin' there above the asphalt plain
I watched another load go to the border
carried by a commuter train
on electric rails of order.

The sky was narrowed the blue-steel grid
and the only mountains I could see
were somewhere behind my left eyelid.
And then I closed my normal entry.

I went thru the revolving door,
unsure about the exit,
and caught the silver tube to my other house
as I wondered 'bout the next set
we would see.

Once I arrived I went immediately for magic smoky air
and I began to look for traces
of explosions in her underwear.
Sniffin' all the places.
Nose open wider than from here to there.
Yes it was wider than from here to there.

I thought about the world thru a backdoor screen
and resumed my independence day.
Slowly I rode that old travellin' train
and watched you/her pass again.

Finally all the children arrived
and they all had their mommas in tow.
Flags began to close off the sky
as they waited on the grassy knoll.
Yes they waited on the grassy knoll
beside the high school.

All eyes were turned to the sky
so I worked my way patiently higher.
They all had their heads turned up
lookin' for my fire.
They were wantin' me to get higher.

At last I could not hold back
and my body shook off somewhere.
I began explodin' and the crowd began to gasp for air.
They *oooohhhddd* and then they *aaaaaahhhddd*.

Yes they *oooooohhhddd* and then they *aaaaaahhhddd*.
Then they *aaaaaahhhddd* and then they *oooooohhhddd*.
And then they *UUNNGHD!*

And I hoped you would be home soon babe.
Can't stand for you to be away.
Come on home America.
Ain't got nobody else to play!
Come on home America.
Can't you see I been waitin' all day!

Well some people called it psychedelic
and others called it 4th of July.
Some people called it a great way to live
and others a great way to die.
The smell of burnt powder filled the air
and fireflies lit the way
as I wondered 'bout revolution
strangely satisfied with my day
of mere little explosions
as I wondered if the feelin' would stay.
Yes I wondered if the feelin' would stay.
Yes I wondered if the feelin' would stay.

At the convenience store

on Jefferson and Joplin
a boy and a girl
maybe 15, open-faced,
buy a Dr. Pepper
and a Coke.

A song blares on the radio.
The girl sings along,
   Oh hell yeah! Oh hell yeah!

Outside,
the summer air
echoes a sweet,
lonely
day in 1965
at Blue Sea strip pit,
the Kotzman Brothers,
eyes innocent,
smiles dreamy,
singing along
with my AM transistor radio,
   I can't get no ... satisfaction,
   I can't get no ... satisfaction,
   but I try, and I try, and I try and I try!

it's funny

how you never
really appreciate
electronic devices
until they die

my smartphone died today

i really appreciate it

It Helps To Get It Out

Today is the first day of Autumn.
I went out to tell the trees that Winter is coming
but, of course, they already knew.
They did ask what was really on my mind
so I told them my brother had asked
a question about my Summer and I was
just getting started by talking about
something else.
It helps to get it out.
Truth is, I'm glad Summer is ending,
the Kansas air so jammed with heat and
humidity that it's like living inside a fever
for months on end.
A kind of deranged flickering around me
as I look out for something cool
to return. A shadow maybe?
Once, while in this state, I called
my departed poet friend, Millo, and asked him
what it's like to be dead.
He said it was like a good edit.
The trees seemed to understand that.

Graveyard Shift At Ace's Truck Stop

Speed popping, long haul truckers stretch, yak, and
drink coffee with locals searching for pancakes or bacon
and eggs after a night of drinking, dancing, gambling, and
making whoopee at nightspots like the Tower Ballroom,
Saddlehead Sam's, the 69 Drive-In, Barto's Idle Hour
and the VFW. The haggard and the high class together.
No place else open. Roy Orbison belts out *Candy Man*
from the neon and chrome Wurlitzer. Cigarette smoke
curls around the horseshoe bar beneath a large, stuffed
deer head. Three a.m., crowd gone, fry cook leans over a
newspaper. Waitress rolls a nickel from her tip pocket
into the juke, punches in her selection, slides wearily
into a booth, puts her feet up, and lights a Pall Mall. Elvis
begins to sing. She closes her eyes and mouths the words,
Are you lonesome tonight? Do you miss me tonight?
Are you sorry we drifted apart?

Bicentennial Laundromat

Here we have our birthday
at the all-american, coin-operated laundromat
and I sit surrounded by speed queens
(those mechanical ladies of american cleanliness)
as a yankee doodle, the perfect american,
tattooed, cigar smoking dandy in a straw hat
eyes meself as he methodically selects
the fitting queen for his 4th of July washout
as the soapy tears inch down
to the dirty checkered floor.
And someone's mother forlornly stuffs
her family's weekly into another queen
while I watch her children riding
in wheeled clothes baskets
and sit cross-legged
waiting for my final rinse.

We are the americans in durable press
staring thru the plate glass world
into the empty eyes of passing redbloods
in an endless stream
pushing their way to find one day's freedom
in a morning parade or explosion in the night.

We do what we did last sunday
helpless to do anything but wash last week away
and wonder where are the t.v. cameras
to transmit our celebration of oxydol
and american bicentennial miracles of mundanity.

Lazarus

Kevin had something of a misconception about the Trappist monks before visiting them for a retreat at a monastery in the Missouri Ozarks.

He imagined they served God by trapping — beaver, rabbit, coyote, raccoon, fox — while living in the depths of the wilderness, only occasionally appearing amid the haunts of civilization with their packs of furs.

He thought: I could do that — wear a white, hooded robe and black cowl. Eat fresh rabbit and squirrel. Live in a cloister at night while running traps and snares in the rolling hills by day.

So imagine his chagrin when he learned they were vegetarian, baked and sold fruitcakes, prayed six times a day and chanted psalms. Drove to Walmart weekly for food and kitchen supplies.

Yet he stayed on, immersed himself into the life, and by the time he entered the novitiate, the chop, chop, chop of the helicopter blades that bent the grass at Ia Drang had given way to the gentle whirr of the ceiling fan that moved the scented air in the half light of the chapel.

I asked him one evening, as he gathered up the pots after supper in the guesthouse, why he'd chosen the professed name of Lazarus. *Because, he responded, before I came here I was dead.*

A couple of years later he left; drove away in a Buick one hot, August afternoon with a nice-looking brunette from Springfield who'd come to the abbey on retreat.

Yep. Just took off. Left everything behind, Father Ted said with a wry smile, *except the name, I guess.*

Centering Prayer

I entered the thick darkness
to dance with God
as the great white bird circled,
his wings across the shadows
of saints and sinners alike.
It was like waking from a dream
of waking from a dream
to find myself next to a sensuous
dark woman as light poured
in filling the room until
it exploded inward on itself.
Like hearing Bird on the sax
going deeper and deeper
inside the music,
becoming music,
becoming God's own jazz of it all,
everything at once flowing
over the reed and out through
the great valved horn.
It was like the Sacred Heart
beatin' the beat
of monks and Mingus alike
   the diaphany of the divine
eros of it all!
It was fidelity and surprise.
It was the Christ in me,
body and blood,
rhythm and blues
just goin' on and doin'
what it needs to.
   Yeahh! as Thomas Merton said
when hearing jazz from his chair.
   Yeahh, now that's prayer!

Raiding The Kitchen At Assumption Abbey

Awoke in full moon
light slanting
down dim hall
while monks
did the big zzzz
and dreamt of
the floating Marygod.

Al jumped high
when I sd, *hey!*
in a low breathburst
& he turned so quickly
he juggled his monkbread
and peanut butter mid
night communion/body
of it all and we pulled free more
milk bread jam
& peanut butter.

Guggle giggle chant/choke
as the milk overshot
and splashed the
shadowed floor.
Al smiled & swiped
as I knelt and ate
a peanut butter
prayer.

You Gotta Call Me

You can call me Higher Power ... *but you gotta call me.*

You can call me God, Lord, Jehovah, Yahweh, The King of Kings, The Lord of Lords, The Almighty, The Supreme Being, The Absolute, The First Cause, The Author of All Things, The Creator of All Things ... *but you gotta call me.*

You can call me The Infinite, The Eternal, The All-Powerful, The Omnipotent, The All-Wise, The All-Merciful, The All-Knowing ... *but you gotta call me.*

You can call me God The Father, The Maker, The Creator, The Preserver ... *but you gotta call me.*

You can call me God The Son, Jesus Christ, The Messiah, The Anointed, The Saviour, The Redeemer, The Mediator, The Intercessor, The Advocate, The Judge, The Son of God, The Son of Man, The Only-Begotten, The Lamb of God, The Word ... *but you gotta call me.*

You can call me Logos, The Man of Sorrows, Jesus of Nazareth, King of the Jews, The Son of Mary, The Risen, Immanuel, The King of Glory, The Prince of Peace, The Good Shepherd, The Way ... *but you gotta call me.*

You can call me The Door, The Truth, The Life, The Bread of Life, The Light of the World, The Vine, The True Vine, The Incarnation, The Word Made Flesh ... *but you gotta call me.*

You can call me Brahma, The Supreme Soul, The Essence of the Universe ... *but you gotta call me.*

You can call me Buddha.
You can call me Vishnu.
You can call me Allah.
You can call me Higher Power ... *but you gotta call me.*

Oh yeah ... *you gotta call me.*

You ... gotta call me.

You gotta call ... *me.*

december kansas twilight

hauling wood to front porch
wheelbarrow circles back
to peach sky behind old
white frame garage

brother john shoots basketball
until too dark to see hoop

brother steve
sells christmas trees
below bare bulb

metal chain keeps perfect time
on steel flagpole
in schoolyard

Martyr To Whiskey

Well she tried and she tried to believe him.
And oh how the pain it did burn.
And many's the time she would leave him
But then she would always return.

  We all need someone to take care of
  And pick up each time that they fall.
  Being a martyr to whiskey
  Is better than nothin' at all.

She grew up livin' with drinkin'.
Her dad, he was gone most the time.
Her mother, she turned to religion
And blamed the whole world for the crime.

Her brother left home with the promise,
It'll never, never happen to me.
But the last time they met he was drinkin'
To hide all the pain he can't see.

They yearn and they yearn for their freedom
And hope that their story will change.
But as much as they yearn for their freedom
They all fear they will miss their chains.

A son phones his father to say

he has to leave detox in Wichita,
that there's no treatment beds
and he has no place to go.

Silence lumbers between them
like a diesel switch engine.

He tells his son to look for a mission
or homeless shelter.

That night he wakes up afraid.

For Fowler
with thanks to William Stafford

You are woven into the puzzle
of my heart
the jigsaw I try
and try to put together.

I am afraid
beneath the half moon of early morning
of not finding all the pieces.

I know that something in you hurts
and that you have carried it bravely.
Can you see the shadow on my face
that carries it with you?

News From The Front
December 22, 2015

Brothers and sisters,

Heartbreak of addiction persists. Fowler relapsed. Asked to leave halfway house. We're looking for long-term tx options. Trip to Phoenix canceled. As they say in AA, *cunning, baffling and powerful.* So true ... but they left out *evil*.

Lucky to have Linda to hold on to and love.

Grief and gratitude are what it's all about, Alfie.

Still going out every morning to put brother Bill's compression stocking on. Edema holding at the same size of other foot / ankle. Took him to Dr. last week for rash near scrotum. *Jock itch!* he announced to the waiting room. Supervising the delivery of new La-Z-Boy recliner for him this morning.

Mother Helen's still a rush. As Buddhist nun, Pema Chodron, might say, *She has a high potential to be bothered.* And I have a high potential to be bothered when around her — so she's helping me burn off a little karma first thing every morning.

All in all, I'm managing pretty well — by taking refuge in the Buddha, the Christ and the Carbohydrates.

Much love,

Jaetea

fatherhood

he sighs in brilliant colors

i weep

as they enter my spine

tai chi training continues

on euclid's curve
mathematics professor
walks slowly home to wife

1955 sacred heart
before basketball shot clock
dad stalls, score 10-8

second story christmas star
shining all night
gives hope to ethel

watching dogs play
I lose fear
of losing

teenager turns stereo up
mother sighs / smiles
listens to tom petty
free fallin'

visiting day at county jail
son leaning across green cubicle
for goodbye touch through glass

dog shit in yard
cat puke in house
tai chi training continues

For Him

Dad's 83rd birthday
Morning blushed on the east side of everything for him

March Madness on TV
KU made the Final Four for him

Wheel-chaired to Mass Palm Sunday
Sacred Heart exposed itself for him

In my budding apple tree
Bird blew hosannas for him

Near the low backyard fence
Daffodil trumpeted Miles ballad for him

South to Watts, Oklahoma
Freight train rattled and rolled for him

Deep in Ozark mountain monastery
Trappist monks chanted for him

In the cloister of my heart
Exquisite silence listened for him

Alone in an empty gym
Made seven of ten free throws for him

From Then On

I was eight when my dad came back from Vietnam
wounded in action.
With my crayons
I made a sign
that said MY DAD IS A HERO
and walked the streets of our Wichita neighborhood
tall and proud.
Some guys stopped their car
slapped me around
tore up my sign
called my dad a baby killer.
My mother crushed half a Valium
fed it to me
and told me to stop crying.
A few weeks later, my dad and I
were driving in the car when
he heard a backfire and dove
under the dashboard
trembling
wild-eyed.
He made me promise never to tell anyone.
From then on
I knew
things would never be the same.

Greeting The Fish

Every morning
before breakfast
I greet the fish.

I stroll among them
exchanging madness
in fish language.

Poetry
some call it
this unblinking eye
this gill ever open
to the subtle breath
of water.

These things we share
with grace
passion
like music through the ages
sweet
terrifying
anonymous.

hitchhiking

abstract beauty in the roadside trash
beckons me to the edge

beer can

birth control pill holder

muffler

i stand above the elegant work
and piss a fresh yellow spray
into the frame

my brother wears my right glove for hitchhiking
i wear the left to symbolize the power
of separation

cars *whoosh* by like airbeams
in a vacuum of knowing

Stairway To Brute

Is the stairway a threat?
Would you feel better it were a savage

some brute barbarian
or semi-barbarian brute
to confront
in an open field?

Is it the stairway
or the steps?

When was the last time
you kissed some brute
full on the red lips
and slept in fear of waking
to find it gone?

i'm not miro, nor chagall

i'm not miro, nor chagall
but I like to watch angels wrestle, especially in kansas
with milky catalpa blossoms falling slow motion
to the red brick sidewalks

why am i telling you this?

because you live in those catalpa blossoms
and because another rainy evening finds
me on the ephemeral edge
thinking about walt whitman
who so loved leaves
that he gave his life
for them

i saw stevie pallucca

pedaling hard against the south wind
on his old red fat
tired bicycle

muse
on the back fender
whispering

face
full of wonder
and puzzlement

heart
spinning
at 1 : infinity

Borderline Song

for Edgewater-Uptown Mental Health

What is to be expected when there is no borderline?
What is to be distinguished
when you can't find space and time?
And the freedom of insanity lures like a golden star.
In the sweet depths of humanity,
do you know who you are?

> I'm just alone and hungry.
> Please don't judge me insane.
> Can't you see the absurdity
> of keepin' up this way?
> My mind gets lost in places
> where demons dance and shout.
> I'm just lookin' for a solid wall
> to feel my way back out.

You know we're not so different, my friend you and I.
You have got your madness, and I sure as hell got mine.
Only mine has a definition,
and yours is yet to be revealed
for fear of its contagiousness
in truth beneath your shield.

So don't channel me by consensus into not being free
to explore the world of my fantasy
and find what I can be.
Don't try to make me wonder
if I should do it your way.
Just listen to my story
and say you'll let me stay.

Haircut

Now I like flowers
and a new-mowed lawn
but there's something about a good stand of weeds
in late Kansas summer

full of grasshoppers
spinning off in all directions

as I advance.

I stand
clutching at hair
groping for space.

When there seems no way to cry out
the grass grows.

Running Away Down A Dead End Street (A Psychotherapist's Guide)

One
Every day begins
with a sensuous kiss.

Makes no difference
about their breath
or the hair
upon their face.

Every day
I wake with a new brute
waiting lovingly
for my morning caress

and I must kiss.

Two
Blackbirds are singing
high on the roots
of my catalpa.

A jackal crosses the yard
nose to the ground
molecules curving colorless
into his gaping nostrils.

My son screams
causing the radio to switch on.

The first message is from Washington
where they are watching
the situation closely.
Death takes my hand
and whispers
brilliant words.

Three
My paperboy is lost somewhere.

I knew it would happen.
I knew all this would happen,
    that he would become lost
    in the capital W of words
        the blackbirds
the jackal
the whispers.

His bicycle wheels
have grown
too large for my street.
He sits by the water
watching the red sails
move away.

Epilogue
There is no difference
between the anxiety I feel
when I face the world
of sliced time
and when I return to poetry.
When I am anxious
I am in the doorway.

KEEP MOVING
or
JUST SIT DOWN ON THE STEPS.

Accept it.
Be ready
to see something.

J.T. KNOLL

Former co-owner of White Buffalo Café and Emporium and founding member of White Buffalo, J.T. Knoll has twice been awarded first place in column writing by The Kansas Press Association as a columnist for *The Morning Sun*. He has performed original songs and poetry in a myriad of venues across the country and led mindfulness and training workshops throughout the Midwest. His poetry has appeared in journals such as *The Midwest Quarterly, Another Chicago Magazine, Chameleon*, and *The Little Balkans Review*. His published collections include *Paperboy, True Stories, Entry / Exit Point, Chorus Line, Where The Pavement Ends*, and *Fetch Crazy*. He lives with his wife, Linda, and Arlo the Labradorian on Euclid's curve in Pittsburg, Kansas, where he operates Knoll Training and Consulting. An ambivert, he is equally at home meditating and reading in his room as singing and reciting poetry in a performance hall.

Acknowledgments from the Author

Some of these poems and songs were previously published in the following publications: *Another Chicago Magazine, Tortilla, Chameleon, The Little Balkans Review, The Midwest Quarterly, Wind, Man!, The Morning Sun, Paperboy, Chorus Line, Moravagine3, Where The Pavement Ends, Entry / Exit Point*, and *Nashville's Poetry Magazine*. I'm high-tingled about sharing these pages with my fellow White Buffaloes (Melissa, Adam, and Al) and want to offer a special thanks to Jason Ryberg, Spartan Press, and 39 West Press for bringing this book to publication. Thanks also to Gene DeGruson, Joe Speer, and John Knoll, my brother, for their poems and inspiration and special thanks to my little bride and muse, Linda, for listening, editing, and dancing rock and roll with me in the kitchen.

ACKNOWLEDGMENTS

This book was published by 39 West Press in partnership with Spartan Press.

Spartan Press would like to thank Prospero's Books, Jeanette Powers, Shawn Pavey, Shaun Savings, Jesse Kates, Jim Holroyd, Steven H. Bridgens, Thomas Mason, Beth Dille, Mason Wolf, Katherine Samet, The Prospero Institute of Disquieted P/O/E/T/I/C/S, The West Plaza Tomato Co., The Fellowship of N-Finite Jest, and The Robert J. Deuser Foundation for Libertarian Studies.

Photo Credits

Tower Café and Ballroom (front cover). Courtesy of Ron & Jeanell Lipasek. *Scenes of Pittsburg, Kansas*: http://pittsburgksmemories.com/.

Grimaldi's Dog Food (p. 3), Sandella's Laundry (p. 99), and Downtown Pittsburg, KS (p. 196-197). Courtesy of Janette Mauk. Axe Library Special Collections, Pittsburg State University.

Sell & Son's Hardware (p. 59) and A.J. Cripe Town Talk Bread (p. 133). Courtesy of Katharine Stelle Spigarelli.

www.ingramcontent.com/pod-product-compliance
Lightning Source LLC
Chambersburg PA
CBHW020613300426
44113CB00007B/624